BARRON'S

COMMON CORE SUCCESS

LEARN, REVIEW, APPLY

GRADE 5 MATH

Tina Pfeiffer

Consulting Editor

Credits: Title page, ©Lisa F. Young /Shutterstock, Pages 4-9, Common Core State Standards, © Copyright 2010. National Governors Association Center for Best Practices and Council of Chief State School Officers. All rights reserved; Page 5 ©Sergey Novikov/Shutterstock, Page 9 ©Sergey Novikov/Shutterstock Page 10 ©Sergey Novikov/Shutterstock, Page 12 (girl) ©Syda Productions/Shuttestock (cds) ©Mariano N. Ruiz/Shutterstock, Page 13 ©ANATOL/Shutterstock, Page 15 ©Ruslan Guzov/Shutterstock, Page 16 ©2xSamara.com/Shutterstock, Page 21 ©Fetullah Mercan/Shutterstock, Page 24 ©Samuel Borges Photography/Shutterstock, Page 25 ©Ivonne Wierink/Shutterstock, Page 26 ©Sergey Novikov/Shutterstock, Page 27 ©auremar/Shutterstock, Page 28 ©Sergey Novikov/Shutterstock, Page 31 ©Sergey Novikov/Shutterstock, Page 32 ©(boy) milias1987/Shutterstock, (girl) Ijansempoi/Shutterstock, Page 33 ©Carolyn Franks/Shutterstock, Page 35 © Lilu330/Shutterstock, Page 36 ©Sergey Novikov/Shutterstock, Page 40 ©Simon Greig/Shutterstock, Page 45 ©Colorlife/Shutterstock, Page 47 ©tanatat/Shutterstock, Page 48 ©Vorobyeva/Shutterstock, Page 50 (scissors) ©motorolka/Shutterstock, (girl) ©akvafoto2012/Fotolia, Page 51 ©Sergey Novikov/Shutterstock, Page 53 (girls with computer) ©Jaimie Duplass/Shutterstock, (cards) © Maryna Yakovchuk/Shutterstock, Page 58 ©ineartestpilot/Shutterstock, Page 58 ©ineartestpilot/Shutterstock, Page 61 ©hvoya/Shutterstock, Page 62 ©photastic/Shutterstock, Page 63 ©freesoulproduction/Shutterstock, Page 65 ©Sergey Novikov/Shutterstock, Page 66 ©RTimages/Shutterstock, Page 67 ©Sirirak Kaewgom/Shutterstock, Page 69 ©Eve's Food Photography/Shutterstock, Page 70 ©Celig/Shutterstock, Page 71 ©Planner/Shutterstock, Page 72 ©eurobanks/Shutterstock, Page 77 ©Andrey Lobachev/Shutterstock, Page 78 ©5 second Studio/Shutterstock, Page 79 ©Koraysa/Shutterstock, Page 80 ©EM Arts/Shutterstock, Page 81 © STILLFX/Shutterstock, Page 82 ©Rob/Shutterstock, Page 84 ©Dean Drobot/Shutterstock, Page 85 ©erentz Agnes/Shutterstock, Page 87 ©aperturesound/Shutterstock, Page 93 ©Moving Moment/Shutterstock, Page 95 ©soloir/Shutterstock, Page 96 ©vvoe/Fotolia, Page 97 ©Barry Blackburn/Shutterstock, Page 99 © Susan Schmitz/Shutterstock, Page 104 ©Veronica Louro/Shutterstock, Page 105 ©Binh Thanh Bui/Shutterstock, Page 106 ©JoHo/Shutterstock, Page 109 ©ImEverything/Shutterstock, Page 110 ©vivanm/Shutterstock, Page 112 ©Thermchai/Shutterstock, Page 113 ©SergiyN/Shutterstock, Page 114 ©Olesya Feketa /Shutterstock Page 119 ©Valentyna Chukhlyebova/Shutterstock, Page 120 ©donnacoleman/Fotolia, Page 121 ©dule964/Fotolia, Page 124 © Scott Griessel/Fotolia, Page 126 ©andriigorulko/Fotolia, Page 130 © 5 second Studio/Shutterstock Page 132 ©Matthew Cole/Shutterstock, Page 134 ©MAHATHIR MOHD YASIN/Shutterstock, Page 136 ©sijohnsen/Shutterstock, Page 137 ©michaeljung/Shutterstock, Page 140 ©Gelpi JM/Shutterstock, Page 141 ©NEGOVURA/Shutterstock, Page 142 ©Kamira'/Shutterstock, Page 143 ©geographlo/Shutterstock, Page 145 ©crysrob/BigStockPhoto Page 146 © SergiyN/Shutterstock, Page 147 ©Danijela Radakovic/Shutterstock, Page 148 ©Fetullah Mercan/Shutterstock Page 149 ©wanphen chawarung/Shutterstock, Page 151 ©Dora Zett/Shutterstock, Page 152 ©Ian 2010/Shutterstock, Page 154 ©Nerthuz/Shutterstock, Page 155 ©Funny Solution Studio/Shutterstock, Page 156 ©Yuriy Rudyy/Shutterstock, Page 159 ©Vinicius Tupinamba/Shutterstock, Page 160 ©Grounder/Shutterstock, Page 161 ©Planner/Shutterstock Page 162 ©Dimitr/Shutterstock, Page 166 ©Monkey Business/Fotolia

BARRON'S

The recent adoption of the Common Core Standards now provides a distinct path to mathematic success. The standards are clear, the performance expectations are high, and the need for problem-solving is rigorous. The transition to this new method has been demanding for teachers, students, and parents alike. As a matter of fact, many parents, tutors, and even older siblings often think, "We never did it this way!"

Charged with the task of creating a parent-friendly mathematics handbook, we realized this was our opportunity to become the support that is critically needed. As classroom teachers for over forty-six years collectively, we have worked collaboratively for a number of years to improve our math instructional practices. Our math instruction evolved as a result of many research projects conducted within our classrooms. Using this research, we developed innovative ways to teach concepts otherwise viewed as extremely difficult by our students. We know what has to be taught, and we understand the struggles that students experience as they strive to achieve mastery.

The new Common Core Standards call for higher-level thinking and in-depth application of math content in multi-step word problems. Along with Common Core content standards, there are eight practice standards that dictate the behaviors required of our students as they engage in mathematics. As a result, we have implemented our **Ace It Time!** activity, or what Van de Walle refers to as a "math-rich" problem for each lesson. This is a rubric or checklist that will guide each student in the problem-solving process. It will also challenge him or her to explain his or her own thinking. This is often an element missing within most home resources. Parents will be able to turn to our product for support, insight, and assistance. They will have an invaluable resource that explains the standards in parent-friendly language, outlines the task required for that standard, teaches it in an easy-to-understand way, and provides adequate opportunities for practice. You will find that resource in our Barron's Common Core Success Math Series.

Parents, teachers, tutors, and other homework helpers—we wish you much success in your journey to help your student master the Common Core!

Jessica Snyder, M.Ed.

Introduction to Problem Solving and Mathematical Practices

This book will help to equip both students and parents with strategies to solve math problems successfully. Problem solving in the mathematics classroom involves more than calculations alone. It involves a student's ability to consistently show his or her reasoning and comprehension skills to model and explain what he or she has been taught. These skills will form the basis for future success in meeting life's goals. Working through the Common Core State Standards each year through the twelfth grade sets the necessary foundation for collegiate and career success. Your student will be better prepared to handle the challenges that await him or her as he or she gradually enters into the global marketplace.

Fluency With Whole Numbers and Decimals

Place Value, Multiplication, and Expressions

CCSS.MATH.CONTENT.5.OA.A.1 – Use parentheses, brackets, or braces in numerical expressions, and evaluate expressions with these symbols.

CCSS.MATH.CONTENT.5.OA.A.2 – Write simple expressions that record calculations with numbers, and interpret numerical expressions without evaluating them. For example, express the calculation "add 8 and 7, then multiply by 2" as 2 × (8 + 7). Recognize that 3 × (18932 + 921) is three times as large as 18932 + 921, without having to calculate the indicated sum or product.

CCSS.MATH.CONTENT.5.NBT.A.1 – Recognize that in a multi-digit number, a digit in one place represents 10 times as much as it represents in the place to its right and $\frac{1}{10}$ of what it represents in the place to its left.

CCSS.MATH.CONTENT.5.NBT.A.2 – Explain patterns in the number of zeros of the product when multiplying a number by powers of 10, and explain patterns in the placement of the decimal point when a decimal is multiplied or divided by a power of 10. Use whole-number exponents to denote powers of 10.

CCSS.MATH.CONTENT.5.NBT.B.5 – Fluently multiply multi-digit whole numbers using the standard algorithm.

Divide Whole Numbers

CCSS.MATH.CONTENT.5.NBT.B.6 – Find whole-number quotients of whole numbers with up to four-digit dividends and two-digit divisors, using strategies based on place value, the properties of operations, and/or the relationship between multiplication and division. Illustrate and explain the calculation by using equations, rectangular arrays, and/or area models.

CCSS.MATH.CONTENT.5.NF.B.3 – Interpret a fraction as division of the numerator by the denominator ($\frac{a}{b}$ = a ÷ b). Solve word problems involving division of whole numbers leading to answers in the form of fractions or mixed numbers, by using visual fraction models or equations to represent the problem. For example, interpret $\frac{3}{4}$ as the result of dividing 3 by 4, noting that $\frac{3}{4}$ multiplied by 4 equals 3, and that when 3 wholes are shared equally among 4 people each person has a share of size $\frac{3}{4}$. If 9 people want to share a 50-pound sack of rice equally by weight, how many pounds of rice should each person get? Between what two whole numbers does your answer lie?

Add and Subtract Decimals

CCSS.MATH.CONTENT.5.NBT.A.1 – Recognize that in a multi-digit number, a digit in one place represents 10 times as much as it represents in the place to its right and $\frac{1}{10}$ of what it represents in the place to its left.

CCSS.MATH.CONTENT.5.NBT.A.3 – Read, write, and compare decimals to thousandths.

a. Read and write decimals to thousandths using base-ten numerals, number names, and expanded form, e.g., $347.392 = 3 \times 100 + 4 \times 10 + 7 \times 1 + 3 \times (\frac{1}{10}) + 9 \times (\frac{1}{100}) + 2 \times (\frac{1}{1000})$

b. Compare two decimals to thousandths based on meanings of the digits in each place, using >, =, and < symbols to record the results of comparisons.

CCSS.MATH.CONTENT.5.NBT.A.4 – Use place value understanding to round decimals to any place.

CCSS.MATH.CONTENT.5.NBT.B.7 – Add, subtract, multiply, and divide decimals to hundredths, using concrete models or drawings and strategies based on place value, properties of operations, and/or the relationship between addition and subtraction; relate the strategy to a written method and explain the reasoning used.

Multiply and Divide Decimals

CCSS.MATH.CONTENT.5.NBT.A.2 – Explain patterns in the number of zeros of the product when multiplying a number by powers of 10, and explain patterns in the placement of the decimal point when a decimal is multiplied or divided by a power of 10. Use whole-number exponents to denote powers of 10.

CCSS.MATH.CONTENT.5.NBT.B.7 – Add, subtract, multiply, and divide decimals to hundredths, using concrete models or drawings and strategies based on place value, properties of operations, and/or the relationship between addition and subtraction; relate the strategy to a written method and explain the reasoning used.

Operations with Fractions

Add and Subtract Fractions with Unlike Denominators

CCSS.MATH.CONTENT.5.NF.A.1 – Add and subtract fractions with unlike denominators (including mixed numbers) by replacing given fractions with equivalent fractions in such a way as to produce an equivalent sum or difference of fractions with like denominators. For example, $\frac{2}{3} + \frac{5}{4} = \frac{8}{12} + \frac{15}{12} = \frac{23}{12}$

(In general, $\frac{a}{b} + \frac{c}{d} = \frac{ad + bc}{bd}$)

CCSS.MATH.CONTENT.5.NF.A.2 – Solve word problems involving addition and subtraction of fractions referring to the same whole, including cases of unlike denominators, e.g., by using visual fraction models or equations to represent the problem. Use benchmark fractions and number sense of fractions to estimate mentally and assess the reasonableness of answers. For example,

recognize an incorrect result such as $\frac{2}{5} + \frac{1}{2} = \frac{3}{7}$, by observing that $\frac{3}{7} < \frac{1}{2}$

Multiply and Divide Fractions

CCSS.MATH.CONTENT.5.NF.B.3 – Interpret a fraction as division of the numerator by the denominator ($\frac{a}{b} = a \div b$). Solve word problems involving division of whole numbers leading to answers in the form of fractions or mixed numbers, by using visual fraction models or equations to represent the problem. For example, interpret $\frac{3}{4}$ as the result of dividing 3 by 4, noting that $\frac{3}{4}$ multiplied by 4 equals 3, and that when 3 wholes are shared equally among 4 people each person has a share of size $\frac{3}{4}$. If 9 people want to share a 50-pound sack of rice equally by weight, how many pounds of rice should each person get? Between what two whole numbers does your answer lie?

CCSS.MATH.CONTENT.5.NF.B.4 – Apply and extend previous understandings of multiplication to multiply a fraction or whole number by a fraction.

a. Interpret the product $(\frac{a}{b}) \times q$ as a parts of a partition of q into b equal parts; equivalently, as the result of a sequence of operations a × q ÷ b. For example, use a visual fraction model to show $(\frac{2}{3}) \times 4 = \frac{8}{3}$, and create a story context for this equation. Do the same with $(\frac{2}{3}) \times (\frac{4}{5}) = \frac{8}{15}$ (In general, $(\frac{a}{b}) \times (\frac{c}{d}) = \frac{ac}{bd}$)

b. Find the area of a rectangle with fractional side lengths by tiling it with unit squares of the appropriate unit fraction side lengths, and show that the area is the same as would be found by multiplying the side lengths. Multiply fractional side lengths to find areas of rectangles, and represent fraction products as rectangular areas.

CCSS.MATH.CONTENT.5.NF.B.5 – Interpret multiplication as scaling (resizing) by:

a. Comparing the size of a product to the size of one factor on the basis of the size of the other factor, without performing the indicated multiplication.

b. Explaining why multiplying a given number by a fraction greater than 1 results in a product greater than the given number (recognizing multiplication by whole numbers greater than 1 as a familiar case); explaining why multiplying a given number by a fraction less than 1 results in a product smaller than the given number; and relating the principle of fraction equivalence $\frac{a}{b} = \frac{(n \times a)}{(n \times b)}$ to the effect of multiplying $\frac{a}{b}$ by 1.

CCSS.MATH.CONTENT.5.NF.B.6 – Solve real-world problems involving multiplication of fractions and mixed numbers, e.g., by using visual fraction models or equations to represent the problem.

CCSS.MATH.CONTENT.5.NF.B.7 – Apply and extend previous understandings of division to divide unit fractions by whole numbers and whole numbers by unit fractions.

a. Interpret division of a unit fraction by a non-zero whole number, and compute such quotients. For example, create a story context for $(\frac{1}{3}) \div 4$, and use a visual fraction model to show the quotient. Use the relationship between multiplication and division to explain that $(\frac{1}{3}) \div 4 = \frac{1}{12}$ because $(\frac{1}{12}) \times 4 = \frac{1}{3}$

b. Interpret division of a whole number by a unit fraction, and compute such quotients. For example, create a story context for $4 \div (\frac{1}{5})$, and use a visual fraction model to show the quotient. Use the relationship between multiplication and division to explain that $4 \div (\frac{1}{5}) = 20$ because $20 \times (\frac{1}{5}) = 4$.

c. Solve real-world problems involving division of unit fractions by non-zero whole numbers and division of whole numbers by unit fractions, e.g., by using visual fraction models and equations to represent the problem. For example, how much chocolate will each person get if 3 people share $\frac{1}{2}$ lb of chocolate equally? How many $\frac{1}{3}$-cup servings are in 2 cups of raisins?

Geometry and Measurement

Patterns and Graphing

CCSS.MATH.CONTENT.5.MD.B.2 – Make a line plot to display a data set of measurements in fractions of a unit $(\frac{1}{2}, \frac{1}{4}, \frac{1}{8})$. Use operations on fractions in this grade to solve problems involving information presented in line plots. For example, given different measurements of liquid in identical beakers, find the amount of liquid each beaker would contain if the total amount in all the beakers were redistributed equally.

CCSS.MATH.CONTENT.5.G.A.1 – Use a pair of perpendicular number lines, called axes, to define a coordinate system, with the intersection of the lines (the origin) arranged to coincide with the 0 on each line and a given point in the plane located by using an ordered pair of numbers, called its coordinates. Understand that the first number indicates how far to travel from the origin in the direction of one axis, and the second number indicates how far to travel in the direction of the second axis, with the convention that the names of the two axes and the coordinates correspond (e.g., x-axis and x-coordinate, y-axis and y-coordinate).

CCSS.MATH.CONTENT.5.G.A.2 – Represent real-world and mathematical problems by graphing points in the first quadrant of the coordinate plane, and interpret coordinate values of points in the context of the situation.

CCSS.MATH.CONTENT.5.OA.B.3 – Generate two numerical patterns using two given rules. Identify apparent relationships between corresponding terms. Form ordered pairs consisting of corresponding terms from the two patterns, and graph the ordered pairs on a coordinate plane. For example, given the rule, "Add 3," and the starting number 0, and given the rule, "Add 6," and the starting number 0, generate terms in the resulting sequences, and observe that the terms in one sequence are twice the corresponding terms in the other sequence. Explain informally why this is so.

Convert Units of Measure

CCSS.MATH.CONTENT.5.MD.A.1 – Convert among different-sized standard measurement units within a given measurement system (e.g., convert 5 cm to 0.05 m), and use these conversions in solving multi-step, real-world problems.

Geometry and Volume

CCSS.MATH.CONTENT.5.G.B.3 – Understand that attributes belonging to a category of two-dimensional figures also belong to all subcategories of that category. For example, all rectangles have four right angles and squares are rectangles, so all squares have four right angles.

CCSS.MATH.CONTENT.5.G.B.4 – Classify two-dimensional figures in a hierarchy based on properties.

CCSS.MATH.CONTENT.5.MD.C.3 – Recognize volume as an attribute of solid figures and understand concepts of volume measurement.

a. A cube with side length 1 unit, called a "unit cube," is said to have "one cubic unit" of volume, and can be used to measure volume.

b. A solid figure which can be packed without gaps or overlaps using n unit cubes is said to have a volume of n cubic units.

CCSS.MATH.CONTENT.5.MD.C.4 – Measure volume by counting unit cubes, using cubic cm, cubic in., cubic ft., and improvised units.

CCSS.MATH.CONTENT.5.MD.C.5 – Relate volume to the operations of multiplication and addition and solve real-world and mathematical problems involving volume.

a. Find the volume of a right rectangular prism with whole-number side lengths by packing it with unit cubes, and show that the volume is the same as would be found by multiplying the edge lengths, equivalently by multiplying the height by the area of the base. Represent threefold whole-number products as volumes, e.g., to represent the associative property of multiplication.

b. Apply the formulas $V = l \times w \times h$ and $V = b \times h$ for rectangular prisms to find volumes of right rectangular prisms with whole number edge lengths in the context of solving real-world and mathematical problems.

c. Recognize volume as additive. Find volumes of solid figures composed of two non-overlapping right rectangular prisms by adding the volumes of the non-overlapping parts, applying this technique to solve real-world problems.

Making Sense of the Problem-Solving Process

For students: The eight mathematical practices outlined in the *Common Core State Standards* ask you to make sense of word problems, write word problems with numbers and symbols, and be able to prove when you are right as well as to know when a mistake happened. These eight practices also state that you may solve a problem by drawing a model, using a chart, list, or other tool. When you get your correct answer, you must be able to explain how and why you chose to solve it that way. Every word problem in this workbook addresses at least three of these practices, helping to prepare you for the demands of problem-solving in your fifth grade classroom. The first unit of this book discusses the **Ace It Time!** section of each lesson. **Ace It Time!** will help you master these practices.

While Doing Mathematics You Will...

1. Make sense of problems and become a champion in solving them

- Solve problems and discuss how you solved them
- Look for a starting point and plan to solve the problem
- Make sense (meaning) of a problem and search for solutions
- Use concrete objects or pictures to solve problems
- Check over work by asking, "Does this make sense?"
- Plan out a problem-solving approach

2. Reason on concepts and understand that they are measurable

- Understand numbers represent specific quantities
- Connect quantities to written symbols
- Take a word problem and represent it with numbers and symbols
- Know and use different properties of operations
- Connect addition and subtraction to length

3. Construct productive arguments and compare the reasoning of others

- Construct arguments using concrete objects, pictures, drawings, and actions
- Practice having conversations/discussions about math
- Explain your own thinking to others and respond to the thinking of others
- Ask questions to clarify the thinking of others (How did you get that answer? Why is that true?)
- Justify your answer and determine if the thinking of others is correct

4. Model with mathematics

- Determine ways to represent the problem mathematically
- Represent story problems in different ways; examples may include numbers, words, drawing pictures, using objects, acting out, making a chart or list, writing equations
- Make connections between the different representations and explain
- Evaluate your answers and think about whether or not they make sense

5. Use appropriate tools strategically

- Consider available tools when solving math problems
- Choose tools appropriately
- Determine when certain tools might be helpful
- Use technology to help with understanding

6. Attend to detail

- Develop math communication skills by using clear and exact language in your math conversations
- Understand meanings of symbols and label appropriately
- Calculate accurately

7. Look for and make use of structure

- Apply general math rules to specific situations
- Look for patterns or structure to help solve problems
- Adopt mental math strategies based on patterns such as making ten, fact families, and doubles

8. Look for and express regularity in repeated reasoning

- Notice repeated calculations and look for shortcut methods to solve problems (for example, rounding up and adjusting the answer to compensate for the rounding)
- Evaluate your own work by asking, "Does this make sense?"

For the official Standards of Mathematical Practice, please visit *www.corestandards.org/Math/Practice*.

9

Contents

CORE Problem-Solving Concepts

UNPACK THE STANDARD
You will make sense of word problems and use strategies to solve them.

LEARN IT: You might be asked to work on very difficult problems with many steps. When solving these problems, you should first read the problem, visualize it, and determine what the problem is asking you to do. You should also be able to explain your thinking and use correct vocabulary. Now let's get started on the problem-solving process!

STEP 1: UNDERSTAND

What's the Question?

Math problems in fifth grade can have many steps. Each step is a task on the checklist. First, read the problem and ask yourself, "What question do I have to answer?" and "Will it take more than one step to solve the problem?"

During each **Ace It Time!** section, your first step on the checklist is to find the question that you have to answer and underline it.

Let's Practice: Read the problem below. Ask, "What question do I have to answer?" How many CDs will be on each shelf? Once you identify the question, underline it. Ask, "Will it take more than one step to solve the problem?" No.

Example: Tabitha found a box with 96 CDs in her garage. She must organize these CDs on a bookshelf in the living room. If the bookshelf has 8 shelves and she places an equal number of CDs on each shelf, how many CDs will be on each shelf?

STEP 2: IDENTIFY

What Numbers or Words Are Needed?

It is very important to locate the numbers in your story problem that will help you to solve the problem. Some problems use the word form of a number, and others will use the standard form of a number. After you find the numbers in your story problem, circle them. Let's practice now.

Example: Tabitha found a box with 96 CDs in her garage. She must organize these CDs on a bookshelf in the living room. If the bookshelf has 8 shelves and she places an equal number of CDs on each shelf, then how many CDs will be on each shelf?

ACE IT TIME!

	yes	no
Did you underline the question in the word problem?	○	○
Did you circle the numbers or number words?	○	○
Did you box the supporting details or information needed to solve the problem?	○	○
Did you draw a picture or a graphic organizer and write a math sentence to show your thinking?	○	○
Did you label your numbers and your picture?	○	○
Did you explain your thinking and use math vocabulary words in your explanation?	○	○

ACE IT TIME!

	yes	no
Did you underline the question in the word problem?	○	○
Did you circle the numbers or number words?	○	○
Did you box the supporting details or information needed to solve the problem?	○	○
Did you draw a picture or a graphic organizer and write a math sentence to show your thinking?	○	○
Did you label your numbers and your picture?	○	○
Did you explain your thinking and use math vocabulary words in your explanation?	○	○

STEP 3: RECOGNIZE THE SUPPORTING DETAILS

Name the Operation.

Now let's find the supporting details or important words that will help solve the problem. There are 96 CDs, and you have to put an equal number of CDs on 8 shelves. Put a box around those words.

Think: Are you using addition, subtraction, multiplication, or division to solve this problem? How do you know? You will use division to solve this problem. The supporting details in the problem help you figure this out. There are 96 CDs and Tabitha has to divide them up equally or fair share them onto 8 shelves.

Example: Tabitha found a box with 96 CDs in her garage. She must organize these CDs on a bookshelf in the living room. If the bookshelf has 8 shelves and she places an equal number of CDs on each shelf, then how many CDs will be on each shelf?

ACE IT TIME!

	yes	no
Did you underline the question in the word problem?	yes	no
Did you circle the numbers or number words?	yes	no
Did you box the supporting details or information needed to solve the problem?	yes	no
Did you draw a picture or a graphic organizer and write a math sentence to show your thinking?	yes	no
Did you label your numbers and your picture?	yes	no
Did you explain your thinking and use math vocabulary words in your explanation?	yes	no

STEPS 4–5: SOLVE AND LABEL

It is important that you connect words in your problem to pictures and numbers. Step 4 on the checklist says that you should first draw a picture or a graphic organizer for your problem. Then you can write a math sentence or equation to solve the problem. Finally, label all numbers and pictures in your drawings and work.

Shelf 1	10 + 2	12
Shelf 2	10 + 2	12
Shelf 3	10 + 2	12
Shelf 4	10 + 2	12
Shelf 5	10 + 2	12
Shelf 6	10 + 2	12
Shelf 7	10 + 2	12
Shelf 8	10 + 2	12
Total	80 + 16	96

Number of CDs on each shelf

Number of shelves

Number of CDs to be divided

Example: Tabitha found a box with 96 CDs in her garage. She must organize these CDs on a bookshelf in the living room. If the bookshelf has 8 shelves and she places an equal number of CDs on each shelf, then how many CDs will be on each shelf?

ACE IT TIME!

	yes	no
Did you underline the question in the word problem?	○	○
Did you circle the numbers or number words?	○	○
Did you box the supporting details or information needed to solve the problem?	○	○
Did you draw a picture or a graphic organizer and write a math sentence to show your thinking?	○	○
Did you label your numbers and your picture?	○	○
Did you explain your thinking and use math vocabulary words in your explanation?	○	○

STEP 6: EXPLAIN

Write a Response. Use Math Vocabulary.

You are almost done! Now explain your answer and show your thinking. Write in complete sentences to explain the steps you used to solve the problem. Make sure you use the vocabulary words in the Math Vocabulary box to help you.

Example: Tabitha found a box with 96 CDs in her garage. She must organize these CDs on a bookshelf in the living room. If the bookshelf has 8 shelves and she places an equal number of CDs on each shelf, then how many CDs will be on each shelf?

Sample explanation: I decided to **divide** 96 by 8. I drew a bookshelf with 8 shelves and then began to **fair share** the CDs into each shelf. First, I gave each shelf 10 CDs; that was 80 of the CDs. With 16 left to share, I could put 2 more on each shelf. This gave me a total of 12 CDs on each shelf. I checked my work by multiplying 12 times 8, which is **equal** to 96.

ACE IT TIME!

Math Vocabulary

multiply
divide
fair share
equal

	yes	no
Did you underline the question in the word problem?	○	○
Did you circle the numbers or number words?	○	○
Did you box the supporting details or information needed to solve the problem?	○	○
Did you draw a picture or a graphic organizer and write a math sentence to show your thinking?	○	○
Did you label your numbers and your picture?	○	○
Did you explain your thinking and use math vocabulary words in your explanation?	○	○

Place Value

UNPACK THE STANDARD
You will understand that in multi-digit numbers, moving a digit one place to the left multiplies its value by 10, and moving a digit one place to the right divides its value by 10.

> **LEARN IT:** You count using the base-ten number system. *Base-ten* means that digits increase or decrease ten times in value when you move one place to the left or right. Digits to the left are higher in value. Digits to the right are lower in value.

Example: The value of 1,000 is _____ times as much as the value of 10.

Use blocks to follow the relationship between place and value.

Number	1,000	100	10	1
Model				
Name	cube	flat	long	block

One long has 10 blocks. A long is 10 times as much as a block.

One flat has 10 longs. A flat is 10 times as much as a long.

think! What other patterns do you see in the blocks? How does the place of the 1 digit change from 10 to 1,000?

Use a number line.

Notice that as the positions move to the left, you are multiplying by 10. As the positions move to the right, you are dividing by 10. Dividing by 10 is the same as multiplying by $\frac{1}{10}$.

think!
10 × 10 = 100
10 × 10 × 10 = 1,000
10 × 10 × 10 × 10 = 10,000
10 ÷ 10 = 1
100 ÷ 10 = 10
1,000 ÷ 10 = 100

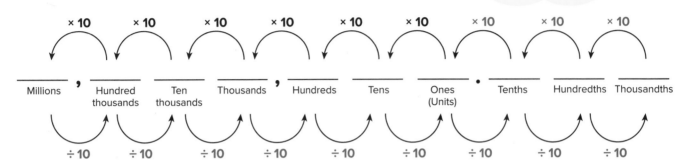

Use a place value chart. Each place value represents a multiple of 10.

Hundred Thousands	Ten Thousands	Thousands	Hundreds	Tens	Ones
100,000	10,000	1,000	100	10	1
			9	5	0
		9	5	0	0

← ——————————— Multiplication

Division ——————————— →

The chart above shows 950 × 10. Multiply by 10 to fill in the spaces to the left of the hundreds place. Divide by 10 to fill in the spaces to the right of the hundreds place.

Notice how the thousands place is 2 spots to the left of the tens place. This is the same as multiplying by 10 twice (10 × 10 = 100).

The value of 1,000 is *100* times as much as the value of 10.

think! When multiplying a whole number, the number gets larger. When dividing a whole number, the number gets smaller.

Standard: CCSS.Math.Content.5.NBT.A.1

PRACTICE: Now you try

Solve the following problems using the methods you just learned.

1. 20 is _____ times as much as 2.	**2.** 3,000 is _____ of 30,000.
3. 560 is 10 times as much as _____.	**4.** 9,500 is $\frac{1}{100}$ of _____.
5. Kendall has 400 songs on her smartphone. Her younger sister has $\frac{1}{10}$ as many songs. How many songs does her younger sister have? _____	**6.** The Banyon County School District has 38,000 elementary students. One-tenth of those students are in extracurricular classes. How many students are in extracurricular classes? _____

Jackson, Devin, and Paulo are having a disagreement in math class. Jackson says that 500,000 is 10 times as much as 50,000. Devin says that 500,000 is 100 times as much as 50,000. Paulo says that 500,000 is $\frac{1}{10}$ of 50,000. Who is correct? How do you know? Show your work and explain your thinking on a piece of paper.

ACE IT TIME!

Math Vocabulary

digit
base ten
place value

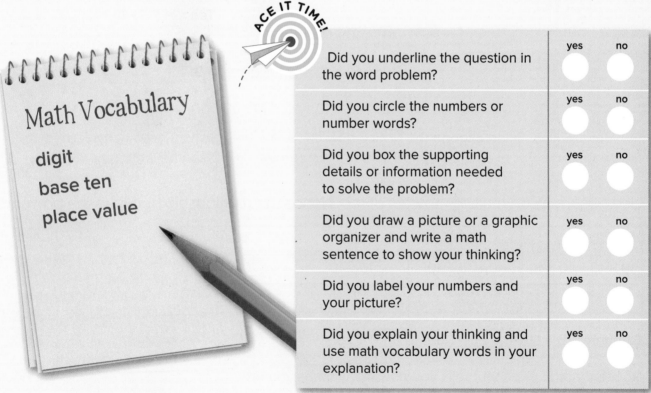

	yes	no
Did you underline the question in the word problem?	◯	◯
Did you circle the numbers or number words?	◯	◯
Did you box the supporting details or information needed to solve the problem?	◯	◯
Did you draw a picture or a graphic organizer and write a math sentence to show your thinking?	◯	◯
Did you label your numbers and your picture?	◯	◯
Did you explain your thinking and use math vocabulary words in your explanation?	◯	◯

MATH ON THE MOVE

Play a game of "What's My Number?" Think of a number. Give clues such as, "I'm thinking of a number that is 100 times greater than 400." Ask an adult or a friend to guess the number. Be sure to discuss how he or she got the answer!

Powers of Ten (Exponents)

UNPACK THE STANDARD
You will be able to explain changes in the number of zeroes or the placement of decimal points when multiplying or dividing by tens, and use exponents to show powers of ten.

LEARN IT: Remember that you count in the base-ten system. Base-ten numbers can be written in different ways to show the *powers of 10.*

Example: Multiply 25 by 1,000.

First write 1,000 as a power of 10.
Here, 10 is the base (or the factor that is multiplied), and 3 is the power (or the number of times the base is multiplied).

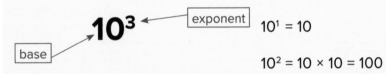

$$10^0 = 1$$

$$10^1 = 10$$

$$10^2 = 10 \times 10 = 100$$

$$10^3 = 10 \times 10 \times 10 = 1,000$$

$$10^4 = 10 \times 10 \times 10 \times 10 = 10,000$$

think! How would you expand 10^6?

Powers are also called **exponents**. Notice how the exponent tells you how many zeroes follow the one. For example, 100 is equal to 1 (no zeroes). 1,000 can be written as 10^3.

Use exponents to multiply powers of ten. Notice the relationship between the powers:

10,000	1,000	100	10
10 × 10 × 10 × 10	10 × 10 × 10	10 × 10	10 × 1
10^4	10^3	10^2	10^1

think! Where is the decimal point in a whole number?
    25 is the same as 25.0 Multiplying by tens moves the decimal point to the right. Dividing by tens moves the decimal point to the left.

Example: $25 \times 1,000 = 25 \times (10 \times 10 \times 10) = 25 \times 10^3 = 25,000$

Notice that the exponent tells you how many times you are multiplying by 10 or how many zeroes to add. Wait! Can you also divide using exponents? Remember that dividing and multiplying are opposite operations.

$25 \div 1,000 = 25 \div (10 \times 10 \times 10) = 25 \div 10^3 = 0.025$

Notice that the exponent tells you how many times you are dividing by 10 or how many places the decimal point moves to the left.

Standard: CCSS.Math.Content.5.NBT.A.1

PRACTICE: Now you try

Use what you know about exponents to find the value of the following expressions.

1. $16 \times 10^2 =$	**2.** $450 \div 10^3 =$
3. $10^3 \times 28 =$	**4.** $47 \div 10^2 =$
5. Courtney scored 450,000 points on her video game. How can she write this number using powers of 10?	**6.** An MP3 player can hold 16,000 songs. How can you write this number using powers of 10?

Casey paid $0.99 for each song she downloaded onto her MP3 player. She bought 10 songs in one month. If she continues to buy 10 songs each month, how much money will she spend on songs in 10 months? Show your work using powers of 10. (*Hint:* First write out the problem without exponents.) Show your work and explain your thinking on a piece of paper.

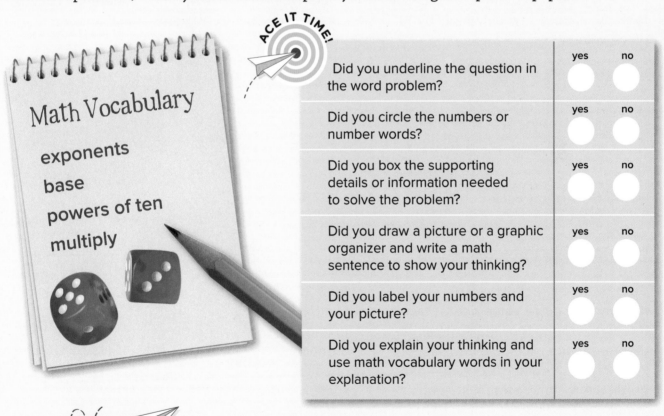

ACE IT TIME!

Math Vocabulary

exponents
base
powers of ten
multiply

	yes	no
Did you underline the question in the word problem?	○	○
Did you circle the numbers or number words?	○	○
Did you box the supporting details or information needed to solve the problem?	○	○
Did you draw a picture or a graphic organizer and write a math sentence to show your thinking?	○	○
Did you label your numbers and your picture?	○	○
Did you explain your thinking and use math vocabulary words in your explanation?	○	○

MATH ON THE MOVE

Roll two dice. Write the first number down. Multiply it by a power of ten. Your second number will be the exponent. For example, if you roll the numbers 3 and 5, solve the problem $3 \times 10^5 = 300,000$.

Multiplication Using Partial Products and Area Models

UNPACK THE STANDARD
You will be able to multiply whole numbers using partial products and area models.

LEARN IT: Partial products and area models both use place value knowledge to multiply numbers.

Example: Multiply 46 by 32.

Solve using partial products.

Step 1: Break each number into expanded form by using place value.

46 = 40 + 6

32 = 30 + 2

Step 2: Multiply each of the parts of 46 by each of the parts of 32 to find the partial products, or parts of the product. Hint: Remember what happens when you multiply by 10: 3 × 4 = 12, so 30 × 40 = 1,200.

		10s	1s
		4	6
	×	3	2

Multiply 30 × 40 ⟶ 1, 2 0 0
Multiply 30 × 6 ⟶ 1 8 0
Multiply 2 × 40 ⟶ 8 0
Multiply 2 × 6 ⟶ + 1 2

1, 4 7 2

Step 3: Add the partial products together to get the final answer.

46 × 32 = 1,472

Use rectangles to break numbers into their parts and multiply with an area model.

Step 1: Draw a rectangle. Break each number into place value parts. Place the parts around the whole rectangle, then break the rectangle into sections. Hint: Because 46 and 32 have 4 parts, break the rectangle into 4 sections.

Step 2: Multiply to find the product of each section.

	40	6
30	30 × 40 1,200	30 × 6 180
2	2 × 40 80	2 × 6 12

Step 3: Add the products together to get the final answer.

```
  1,200
    180
     80
+    12
  1,472
```

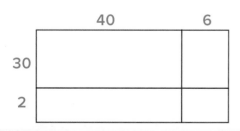

think! How are area models similar to partial products?

Standards: CCSS.Math.Content.5.NBT.A.2, 5.NBT.B.5

PRACTICE: Now you try

Use partial products and the area model to solve the following problems.

1. 95 × 35 =	**2.** 86 × 68 =
3. 146 × 28 =	**4.** 2,463 × 15 =
5. Kali can type 56 words per minute on her laptop. How many words can she type in 45 minutes? *Hint:* How many minutes are in an hour?	**6.** Roberto has 19 folders on his tablet. Each folder contains 23 apps. How many apps does he have on his tablet?

The high-school soccer team is sending 13 team members to the regional meet. Each teammate needs to raise $235 to pay for her expenses. Marley did the math and thinks the team needs a total of $2,055. Kelli thinks the team needs a total of $3,055. Who made an error in her math? Where did she make the error? Show your work and explain your thinking on a piece of paper.

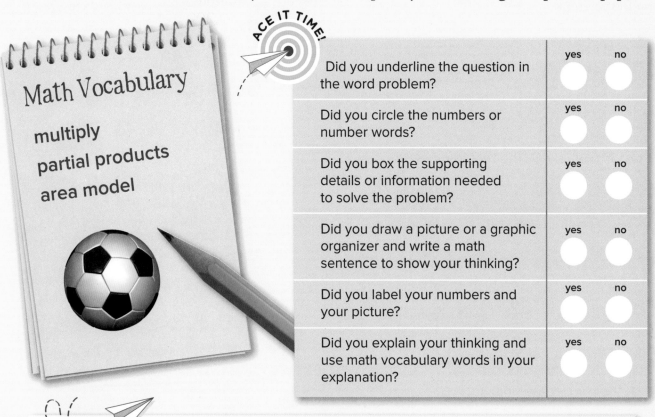

Math Vocabulary

multiply

partial products

area model

ACE IT TIME!

	yes	no
Did you underline the question in the word problem?	○	○
Did you circle the numbers or number words?	○	○
Did you box the supporting details or information needed to solve the problem?	○	○
Did you draw a picture or a graphic organizer and write a math sentence to show your thinking?	○	○
Did you label your numbers and your picture?	○	○
Did you explain your thinking and use math vocabulary words in your explanation?	○	○

MATH ON THE MOVE

Roll the dice two times. Write the first number in the tens place and the second number in the ones place. Repeat to get a second two-digit number. Multiply your two-digit numbers. Solve using any of the strategies you have learned. You can also create and multiply larger numbers!

Multiplication Using the Standard Algorithm

 UNPACK THE STANDARD
You will be able to multiply whole numbers using the standard method of multiplication.

LEARN IT: Use your knowledge of place value and basic multiplication facts to multiply larger numbers with the standard algorithm, or method, of multiplication.

Example: Solve 325 × 46.

Step 1: Write the number in standard form. Remember to line up the numbers by place value.

$$\begin{array}{r} 325 \\ \times\ \ 46 \\ \hline \end{array}$$

Step 2: Multiply by the ones digit of 46. Remember to regroup.

Notice
$$\begin{array}{r} 325 \\ \times\ \ \ 6 \\ \hline 1{,}950 \end{array}$$

$$\begin{array}{r} 3\ \ \ \\ 325 \\ \times\ \ 46 \\ \hline 0 \end{array} \qquad \begin{array}{r} 13\ \ \\ 325 \\ \times\ \ 46 \\ \hline 50 \end{array} \qquad \begin{array}{r} 13\ \ \\ 325 \\ \times\ \ 46 \\ \hline 1{,}950 \end{array}$$

think! Why do you carry the 3 and 1 like we do in addition? When you multiply 5 × 6 = 30, what place value is the 3?
Why do you add the 1 and the 3? Hint: Do partial products and the area model also use addition?

Step 3: Multiply by the tens digit of 46.

think! 40 × 5

think! 40 × 20

think! 40 × 30

$$\begin{array}{r} 2\ \ \ \\ 325 \\ \times\ \ 46 \\ \hline 00 \end{array} \qquad \begin{array}{r} 12\ \ \\ 325 \\ \times\ \ 46 \\ \hline 000 \end{array} \qquad \begin{array}{r} 13\ \ \\ 325 \\ \times\ \ 46 \\ \hline 13{,}000 \end{array}$$

Notice
$$\begin{array}{r} 325 \\ \times\ \ 40 \\ \hline 13{,}000 \end{array}$$

think! Why do you write 2 zeroes in the first step, when 4 × 5 = 20? Hint: What place value is the 4 in 46? Remember your patterns of zeroes.

4 × 5 = 20
40 × 5 = 200

Step 4: Add the products together to get the final answer.

$$\begin{array}{r} 325 \\ \times\ \ 46 \\ \hline 1{,}950 \\ +\ 13{,}000 \\ \hline 14{,}950 \end{array}$$

think! Can you see the similarities between the area model and the standard algorithm when solving 325 × 46?

	300	20	5
40	12,000	800	200
6	1,800	120	30

$$\begin{array}{r} 325 \\ \times\ \ 46 \\ \hline 1{,}950 \\ +\ 13{,}000 \\ \hline 14{,}950 \end{array}$$

Standard: CCSS.Math.Content.5.NBT.B.5

PRACTICE: Now you try

Solve the following problems using the standard algorithm.

1.	56 × 38	**2.**	765 × 43	**3.**	3,047 × 25	**4.**	5,449 × 39

Find the missing digit in the following multiplication problem. Use the standard algorithm, partial products, or area model to help you. Show your work and explain your thinking on a piece of paper.

```
     2 3
  ×  4 ■
  ───────
  1 0 8 1
```

ACE IT TIME!

Math Vocabulary

multiply
place value
product

	yes	no
Did you underline the question in the word problem?	○	○
Did you circle the numbers or number words?	○	○
Did you box the supporting details or information needed to solve the problem?	○	○
Did you draw a picture or a graphic organizer and write a math sentence to show your thinking?	○	○
Did you label your numbers and your picture?	○	○
Did you explain your thinking and use math vocabulary words in your explanation?	○	○

MATH ON THE MOVE

Keep your multiplication facts fast and fresh! Practice with flash cards or games like those found on websites such as *www.multiplication.com*. Ask an adult to give you a basic fact to answer as you enter or leave the room. Continue practicing until you know these facts well.

Expressions

UNPACK THE STANDARD
You will be able to solve expressions using parentheses, brackets, and braces.

LEARN IT: An *expression* is a group of numbers and symbols without an equal sign. Each expression represents a *value*. To find that value, follow the instructions of the symbols (add, subtract, divide, and multiply). There is an *Order of Operations* that mathematicians follow. This is like the rules of grammar when writing. The Order of Operations makes sure each value is calculated correctly.

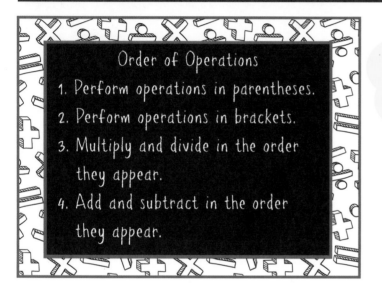

Order of Operations
1. Perform operations in parentheses.
2. Perform operations in brackets.
3. Multiply and divide in the order they appear.
4. Add and subtract in the order they appear.

think! How would math be different without the Order of Operations? How would you know whose answer was correct?

Example: Javier and Sam both solved the expression 5 + 3 × 2, but they got different answers. Look at their explanations and decide who is correct.

Javier's answer: 16	Sam's answer: 11
First, I added 5 + 3 = 8. Next, I multiplied 8 × 2 = 16. So, I think 5 + 3 × 2 = 16.	First, I multiplied 3 × 2 = 6. Next, I added 5 + 6 = 11. So, I think 5 + 3 × 2 = 11.

Sam is correct because he followed the Order of Operations.

Example: Solve the expression: [(3 + 2) − (1 + 1)] × 4 ÷ 3.

Step 1: Solve the parentheses and the brackets.	Step 2: Multiply and divide from left to right.	Step 3: Solve.
[5 − 2] × 4 ÷ 3	3 × 4 ÷ 3	12 ÷ 3 = 4
3 × 4 ÷ 3	12 ÷ 3	So, [(3 + 2) − (1 + 1)] × 4 ÷ 3 = 4

PRACTICE: Now you try

Use the Order of Operations to find the value of the following expressions.

Hint: Parentheses are always placed within brackets

1. $2 + 4 \times 5$	2. $3 \times (4 + 5)$	3. $15 - 3 \div 1$	4. $18 - (2 \times 2) + 1$	5. $[(4 + 1) + (10 \times 2)] \div 5$

A cupcake recipe calls for 2 cups of flour and 1 cup of sugar. If you tripled the recipe, how many cups of these ingredients are needed in all? Write and solve an expression to find the answer. Can you write your expression in a different way? Show your work and explain your thinking on a piece of paper.

ACE IT TIME!

	yes	no
Did you underline the question in the word problem?	◯	◯
Did you circle the numbers or number words?	◯	◯
Did you box the supporting details or information needed to solve the problem?	◯	◯
Did you draw a picture or a graphic organizer and write a math sentence to show your thinking?	◯	◯
Did you label your numbers and your picture?	◯	◯
Did you explain your thinking and use math vocabulary words in your explanation?	◯	◯

Math Vocabulary

expression

multiply

divide

brackets

Order of Operations

parentheses

MATH ON THE MOVE

Create and solve expressions of your own! With a friend or an adult, find two different answers for each expression you create. Debate which answer is correct. Remember, the player who correctly uses the Order of Operations first wins!

Writing Expressions

UNPACK THE STANDARD
You will be able to write simple expressions and understand what they mean without solving them.

LEARN IT: An expression uses symbols to describe the relationships between numbers.

Example: Liam got his $4 allowance twice this month. He also earned $16 painting the fence. How do you describe the total amount of money Liam earned?

Double four and add sixteen.

OR

$2 \times 4 + 16$

think! Remember to use the order of operations! Think about what the symbols in the expression are asking you to do.

Once you understand what the question is, you can look for key words to help you identify the correct operation. Here are some examples:

Addition	Subtraction	Multiplication	Division
sum	difference	product	quotient
plus	less than	times	shared equally
increased by	more than	twice	split up
added to	take away	double	
more	decreased by	each	

PRACTICE: Now you try

Write expressions that match the descriptions below.

1. Subtract 5 from 14 then add 3 multiplied by 2.	**2.** Divide 144 by 12 then multiply by 4 and add 17.
3. James went fishing and caught 4 fish. He threw them back into the pond and then caught 2 more.	**4.** Claire had $20. She spent $8 buying apps for her tablet and $6 on lunch.
5. Jasmine went shopping at 2 different stores. She bought 4 T-shirts that cost $12 each at both stores.	**6.** Mateo had 52 game trading cards. He gave 6 to one friend and 6 to another.

Standard: CCSS.Math.Content.5.OA.A.2

Mr. Young went on a week-long camping trip with his family. Each day, he hiked 4 miles up the mountain and then back down. Mrs. Young also hiked on the trip. She walked a 4-mile trail twice each day. Write an expression for the total miles each walked during the week. What relationship can you see between the two expressions? Show your work and explain your thinking on a piece of paper.

Math Vocabulary

multiply
symbol
operation
expression

ACE IT TIME!

	yes	no
Did you underline the question in the word problem?	◯	◯
Did you circle the numbers or number words?	◯	◯
Did you box the supporting details or information needed to solve the problem?	◯	◯
Did you draw a picture or a graphic organizer and write a math sentence to show your thinking?	◯	◯
Did you label your numbers and your picture?	◯	◯
Did you explain your thinking and use math vocabulary words in your explanation?	◯	◯

MATH ON THE MOVE

Create number riddles and have a partner say or write the matching expression. For example, "Double the sum of 14 and 30" or "Find half of 82 then add 30." For an extra challenge, use mental math to solve the expressions.

Stop and think about what you have learned.

Congratulations! You've finished the lessons for this unit. This means you've learned about place value and powers of ten. You've used different strategies for solving multiplication problems, such as partial products, area models, and the standard algorithm. You've also learned how to solve expressions using the Order of Operations, as well as how to write expressions.

Now it's time to prove your skills with number-system operations. Solve the problems below. Use all of the methods you have learned.

Activity Section 1: Place Value

Solve the following problems using partial products or area model.

1. 34 × ☐ = 3,400	**2.** 340 × ☐ = 340,000
3. 34,000 ÷ ☐ = 340	**4.** 340,000 ÷ ☐ = 340
5. 420 is ☐ times larger than 42.	**6.** 4,200 is ☐ times larger than 42.
7. 42 is $\dfrac{1}{☐}$ of 4,200.	**8.** 42,000 is $\dfrac{1}{☐}$ of 420,000.

Standards: CCSS.Math.Content.5.NBT.A.1, 5.NBT.A.2, 5.NBT.B.5, 5.NBT.B.6, 5.OA.A.1, 5.OA.A.2

Activity Section 2: Powers of Ten

Fill in the boxes to solve the problems.

1. $16 \times 10^{\boxed{}} = 1{,}600$	2. $16 \times 10^{\boxed{}} = 160{,}000$
3. $16{,}000 \div 10^{\boxed{}} = 160$	4. $1{,}600 \div 10^{\boxed{}} = 16$

5. Fill in the blanks to continue the pattern.

$52 \times 10 = 52 \times 10^1 = \boxed{}$

$52 \times 10 \times 10 = 52 \times 10^2 = \boxed{}$

$52 \times 10 \times 10 \times 10 = 52 \times 10^3 = \boxed{}$

$52 \times 10 \times 10 \times 10 \times 10 = \boxed{} = \boxed{}$

$52 \times \boxed{} = 52 \times \boxed{} = \boxed{}$

Activity Section 3: Multiplication Using Partial Products and Area Models

Solve the following problems.

1. Juliet sends 26 texts each day. How many texts does she send in 28 days?	2. A farm grows 15 acres of corn. Each acre produces 285 pounds of corn. How many pounds of corn is that in all?
3. Kim used 264 cubes to construct a tower in her building game. How many cubes would she use to build 23 towers?	4. Clayton drove 2,345 miles each month. How many miles did he drive in one year? *Hint: How many months are in a year?*

Activity Section 4: Multiplication Using the Standard Algorithm

Solve the following problems using the standard algorithm of multiplication.

1. 4,235
  × 6
	2. 5,748
	  × 23
		3. If a cheetah can run 65 miles per hour, how far can it run in 24 hours?

4. A factory can produce 2,585 skateboards in one day. How many skateboards can it produce in 30 days?		**5.** Camden reads 118 words per minute. How many words does he read in 45 minutes?

Activity Section 5: Expressions

Solve the first four problems adding ( ) to find the value. Then, solve the next two problems.

1. Value: 10 22 − 2 + 4 × 2	**2.** Value: 24 48 ÷ 6 × 15 − 12
3. Value: 10 28 − 2 × 3 + 6	**4.** Value: 16 5 + 3 × 4 ÷ 2

5. Marie bought 6 books online at $12 each. She paid a $7 shipping fee. What was the total cost of Marie's order? Choose the expression below that can help you solve the problem.

A. 6 + 12 + 7
B. 6 × 12 + 7
C. 6 × 12 × 7
D. 6 × 7 + 12

6. Which is the correct way to solve 24 − 3 × 6 ÷ 2?

A. 24 − 3 × 6 ÷ 2
  24 − 18 ÷ 2
  6 ÷ 2
  3
	B. 24 − 3 × 6 ÷ 2
	  24 − 3 × 3
	  21 × 3
	  63

C. 24 − 3 × 6 ÷ 2
  24 − 18 ÷ 2
  24 − 9
  15
	D. 24 − 3 × 6 ÷ 2
	  21 × 6 ÷ 2
	  126 ÷ 2
	  63

Standards: CCSS.Math.Content.5.NBT.A.1, 5.NBT.A.2, 5.NBT.B.5, 5.NBT.B.6, 5.OA.A.1, 5.OA.A.2

Activity Section 6: Writing Expressions

Write an expression to match each story.

1. For 4 weeks, Blake earned $14 walking his neighbor's dog and spent $6 a week on music downloads.

_____

2. Lizzie collects 12 seashells each day at the beach for 4 days. She then shares them equally with her little sister.

_____

3. Cameron has $60 saved in his bank account. He spends $18, then gets a check for $15 for his birthday.

_____

4. Dani and her brother are saving up money to buy their father a gift. They both save $5 a week for 6 weeks.

_____

UNDERSTAND

People use numerical expressions to solve math problems all the time. They rely on number sense and operations to help describe and express certain values.

Activity Section

Beth and Corey want to buy a video game. The game costs $45. They both save their $3 allowance for 6 weeks. Write an expression to help them figure out how much money they have saved. Write a second expression showing how much more they need before they can pay for the video game.

Standards: CCSS.Math.Content.5.NBT.B.6; CCSS.Math.Practice.MP1, MP2, MP4, MP6, MP7

Discover how you can apply the information you have learned.

Activity Section

The Scene It movie theater has 4 sections of seats. The middle section has 24 rows with 20 seats in each row. The 2 side sections have 24 rows each but only 8 seats in each row. The back section has 8 rows with 32 seats in each row. How many seats in all does the theater hold?

Show your work and explain your thinking in the space provided.

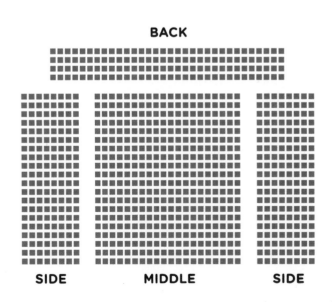

BACK

SIDE   MIDDLE   SIDE

CORE
Division Concepts

Area Model Division

UNPACK THE STANDARD
You will use the area model to divide numbers up to 1,000 by a one-digit divisor.

LEARN IT: Dividing means breaking a whole into smaller groups. It is the opposite of multiplying. In the same way that subtraction uses methods similar to addition, division uses methods similar to multiplication.

Example: Solve 365 ÷ 5. Use an area model.

Step 1: Break the dividend (365) into parts by place value. Choose parts that are multiples of the divisor (5).

365

5	300	60	5

Step 2: Divide each part by the divisor. This will give you partial quotients.

365

5	60 (300 ÷ 5)	12 (60 ÷ 5)	1 (5 ÷ 5)

Step 3: Add the partial quotients.

60 + 12 + 1 = 73

365 ÷ 5 = 73

Sometimes the numbers can't be so easily broken apart. Use your number sense and knowledge of basic facts to find ways to break apart the dividend so that it can be more easily divided by the divisor.

Example: 3,600 ÷ 8 *Hint:* Think of compatible numbers, or numbers that can be divided easily. 36 ÷ 8 is not a basic fact, but 32 ÷ 8 is!

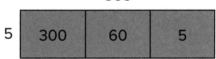

3200 (3200 ÷ 8) 400	400 (400 ÷ 8) 50

⟶ 3,200 + 400 = 3,600

⟶ 400 + 50 = 450

Standard: CCSS.Math.Content.5.NBT.B.6

PRACTICE: Now you try

Use the area model to solve the following. The first one is started for you.

> **think!** Think: Could you also do 300 ÷ 4? Why or why not? Hint: 300 is a multiple of 4.

1. 2,364 ÷ 4 =

2000 (2,000 ÷ 4)	320 (320 ÷ 4)	44 (44 ÷ 4)
_____	_____	_____

_____ + _____ + _____

2. 2,172 ÷ 3 =

Kyle has a recangular patio with an area of 192 square feet. He is buying paving stones that are 1 square foot each. They are sold in boxes of 8. Each box costs $10.00. Kyle's father has saved $400 for the project. Does he have enough money to buy all the paving stones he will need? If not, how much more money does he need? Try using the area model to help you solve. *Hint:* First, figure out how many boxes he will need. Show your work and explain your thinking on a piece of paper.

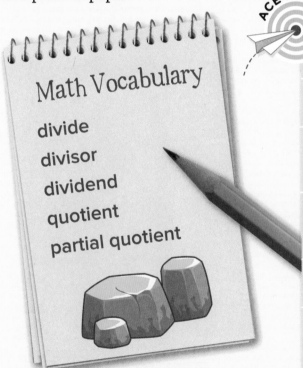

Math Vocabulary

divide
divisor
dividend
quotient
partial quotient

ACE IT TIME!

	yes	no
Did you underline the question in the word problem?	○	○
Did you circle the numbers or number words?	○	○
Did you box the supporting details or information needed to solve the problem?	○	○
Did you draw a picture or a graphic organizer and write a math sentence to show your thinking?	○	○
Did you label your numbers and your picture?	○	○
Did you explain your thinking and use math vocabulary words in your explanation?	○	○

MATH ON THE MOVE

The area model of division requires a solid foundation in place value and breaking apart numbers. Work with an adult. Have the adult give you a random number (a three- or four-digit dividend) to be divided by a one-digit divisor. Think of good "break apart" numbers that work for that dividend and divisor. Remember you can check divisibility rules online at websites such as: *www.studyzone.org/mtestprep/math8/e/divisibilityrules5l.cfm*.

Division with Partial Quotients

UNPACK THE STANDARD
You will divide numbers up to the thousands place by a one-digit divisor.

LEARN IT: The area model breaks the dividend into parts. You can also perform division by finding the quotient in parts. This strategy requires the use of *partial quotients* to divide (see example below).

Example: Solve 6,320 ÷ 5 using partial quotients.

Step 1: Identify the highest place value in the dividend. In 6,320, there are 6 thousands.

Step 2: Use multiplication to find out if there are any thousands in the quotient.

5 × 1,000 = 5,000
5 × 2,000 = 10,000

think! 10,000 is too much! So there is only one group of 5 thousands in 6,320.

Step 3: Subtract the multiple from the dividend.

```
5 ) 6,320
  - 5,000  = 5 × 1,000
    1,320
```

think! You can make 1,000 groups of 5 out of 6,320 because 1,000 × 5 = 5,000.

Step 4: Move to the next lowest place value (hundreds) and repeat.

```
5 ) 6,320
  - 5,000     5 × 1,000
    1,320
  - 1,000     5 × 200
      320
  -   300     5 × 60
       20
  -    20     5 × 4
        0
```

think! The circled numbers are the partial quotients!

Step 5: Add the partial quotients to find the total quotient: **1,000 + 200 + 60 + 4** = 1,264.
So 6,320 ÷ 5 = 1,264.

Standard: CCSS.Math.Content.5.NBT.B.6

PRACTICE: Now you try

Use partial quotients to solve the following.

1. 973 ÷ 7 =	2. 3,969 ÷ 9 =

Sebastian solved the following problem using the partial quotients method of division. But he made an error! Find where he made the error, and correct his mistake. Show your work and explain your thinking on a piece of paper.

$$
\begin{array}{r}
3 \overline{)\,2{,}232} \\
-\,2{,}100 \\
\hline
132 \\
-\,120 \\
\hline
12 \\
-\,12 \\
\hline
0
\end{array}
$$

3 × 700   2,100

3 × 40   120

3 × 1   3

Quotient: **2,223**

ACE IT TIME!

Math Vocabulary

place value

divisor

dividend

quotient

	yes	no
Did you underline the question in the word problem?	○	○
Did you circle the numbers or number words?	○	○
Did you box the supporting details or information needed to solve the problem?	○	○
Did you draw a picture or a graphic organizer and write a math sentence to show your thinking?	○	○
Did you label your numbers and your picture?	○	○
Did you explain your thinking and use math vocabulary words in your explanation?	○	○

MATH ON THE MOVE

Mastering multiples will make long division easier. Ask an adult to help you practice counting and using different multiples. For example, count by 7s or 11s when riding in the car. Count by 15s when doing chores. Race with an adult to see who can count by 8s to 100 the fastest.

Standard Division with One-Digit Divisors

UNPACK THE STANDARD
You will divide numbers up to the thousands place by a one-digit divisor.

LEARN IT: Just like the standard method of multiplication is a shorter way of writing out partial products, the standard method of division is a shorter way of writing out partial quotients.

Example: Solve 6,320 ÷ 5 using the standard method of division.

Step 1: Find the thousands place of the quotient.

think! To find 6,000 ÷ 5, you can think of it as 6 ÷ 5. 6 ÷ 5 = 1 plus some left over so 6,000 ÷ 5 = 1,000 plus some left over.

■ Quotient
■ Product
■ Remainder
■ Dividend
■ Divisor

Step 2: Subtract the product from the dividend to find what's left over (6,000 − 5,000 = 1,000, or 6 − 5 = 1). Move onto the next place.

Step 3: Regroup by dropping the hundreds place down and solve 1,300 ÷ 5 (13 ÷ 5).

Step 4: Subtract the product. Repeat until the divisor no longer goes into the dividend. Identify what's left over as the remainder.

Dirty Monkeys Smell Bad! That phrase can help you remember the order of the steps of long division: Divide, Multiply, Subtract, Bring down!

Standard: CCSS.Math.Content.5.NBT.B.6

PRACTICE: Now you try

Solve the following division problems.

think! Do you need a zero in the hundreds place?

1. $3\overline{)4,542}$

2. $9\overline{)9,540}$

Trey solved the division problem 5,224 ÷ 2 = 11,612. His work is shown below. Can you explain where he made an error? Solve the problem to find the correct answer. Show your work and explain your thinking on a piece of paper.

```
      11,612
   2 ) 5,224
     - 2
       32
     - 32
       02
      - 2
       04
      - 4
        0
```

ACE IT TIME!

	yes	no
Did you underline the question in the word problem?	○	○
Did you circle the numbers or number words?	○	○
Did you box the supporting details or information needed to solve the problem?	○	○
Did you draw a picture or a graphic organizer and write a math sentence to show your thinking?	○	○
Did you label your numbers and your picture?	○	○
Did you explain your thinking and use math vocabulary words in your explanation?	○	○

Math Vocabulary

dividend

divisor

quotient

place value

remainder

Ask an adult to give you simple problems to solve using mental math. For example, try to find the quotient of 420 ÷ 5 without writing anything down. To help you think of simple problems, remember the divisibility rules for 2 and 5 are the easiest. Any even number is divisible by 2, and any number that ends in 0 or 5 is divisible by 5. Visit the following website for the other divisibility rules: *www.studyzone.org/mtestprep/math8/e/divisibilityrules5l.cfm*.

Standard Division with Two-Digit Divisors

UNPACK THE STANDARD
You will divide numbers up to the thousands place by a two-digit divisor.

LEARN IT: Another good way of thinking about division is to ask, "How many groups of (the divisor) can I make out of (the dividend)?"

Example: Solve 2430 ÷ 15 using the standard method of division.

Step 1: Ask, "How many groups of 15 can I make out of 2?"

$$15\overline{)2,430}$$

Because 0 groups of 15 can be made out of 2, move onto the next place value.

Step 2: Ask, "How many groups of 15 can I make out of 24?"

Find multiples of 15 (or count by 15s) to find the answer:

$$
\begin{array}{r}
1 \\
15\overline{)2,430} \\
-15 \\
\hline
93
\end{array}
$$

think! To check your work, compare what's left over after subtraction (9) to the divisor (15). Because 9 < 15, you've found the maximum number of groups of 15 that fit into 24.

Multiples of 15: 15, 30, 45, 60, 75 . . .

You can only make 1 group of 15 out of 24!

Step 3: Move on to the next place value and repeat.

$$
\begin{array}{r}
162 \\
15\overline{)2,430} \\
-15 \\
\hline
93 \\
-90 \\
\hline
30 \\
-30 \\
\hline
0
\end{array}
$$

162 groups of 15 can be made from 2,431.

So 2,430 ÷ 15 = 162

Standard: CCSS.Math.Content.5.NBT.B.6

PRACTICE: Now you try

Solve.

1. 25) 3,625	2. 42) 8,946	3. 24) 5,928

Bryce is helping his father plant vegetables in their garden. They have 1,872 seeds. If they want to plant 39 seeds per row, how many rows can they make? Show your work and explain your thinking on a piece of paper.

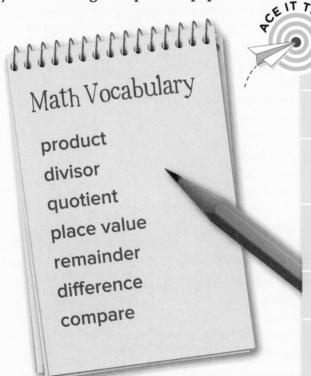

Math Vocabulary

product
divisor
quotient
place value
remainder
difference
compare

ACE IT TIME!

	yes	no
Did you underline the question in the word problem?	○	○
Did you circle the numbers or number words?	○	○
Did you box the supporting details or information needed to solve the problem?	○	○
Did you draw a picture or a graphic organizer and write a math sentence to show your thinking?	○	○
Did you label your numbers and your picture?	○	○
Did you explain your thinking and use math vocabulary words in your explanation?	○	○

MATH ON THE MOVE

Help compute your family car's gas mileage every time your family fills up with gas. Have an adult help you record the numbers you need to do the division. Hint: You'll need to know how many gallons of gas your family bought and how many miles the car has traveled since. Keep a record in the car.

Division with Remainders

UNPACK THE STANDARD
You will use the standard algorithm to divide numbers up to the thousands place and identify remainders.

LEARN IT: Remember your divisibility rules. The number 5 only goes into numbers ending in 0 or 5 (10, 20, 25, and so on). What happens when you want to divide 37 by 5? You will have a *remainder*. A remainder is the amount left over when division is complete.

Remainders can be found using area models, partial quotients, or the standard method. Remember to use your place value knowledge!

Example: Solve 2,552 ÷ 12.

Step 1:

```
      2
12 ) 2,552
    -24↓
      15
```

think! Are there 2 groups of 12 in 2,552 or are there 200? Are you subtracting 24, or are you really subtracting 2,400?

Step 2:

```
     21
12 ) 2,552
    -24
      15
    - 12↓
      32
```

Step 3:

```
    212
12 ) 2,552
    -24
      15
    - 12
      32
    - 24
       8
```

You can take 212 equal groups of 12 out of 2,552 with 8 left over.

Step 4:

```
    212r8
12 ) 2,552
    -24
      15
    - 12
      32
    - 24
       8
```

think! You can't take any groups of 12 out of 8. The remainder is 8. The remainder is always smaller than the divisor.

Try the same problem using partial quotients:

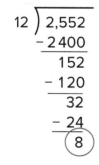

```
12 ) 2,552
    - 2400    200 × 12    200
      152
    - 120     10 × 12      10
       32
    - 24      2 × 12        2
       8              212r8
```

Try it again with the area model:

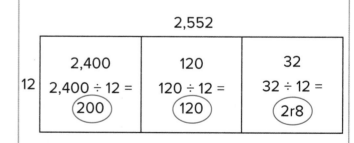

2,552

	2,400	120	32
12	2,400 ÷ 12 = (200)	120 ÷ 12 = (120)	32 ÷ 12 = (2r8)

Standard: CCSS.Math.Content.5.NBT.B.6

PRACTICE: Now you try

Solve.

1. $12 \overline{)1{,}876}$	2. $18 \overline{)6{,}749}$	3. $15 \overline{)5{,}138}$

Matea has 116 pipe cleaners for her art project. She shares them among 8 people. How many pipe cleaners will each person get? Show your work and explain your thinking on a piece of paper.

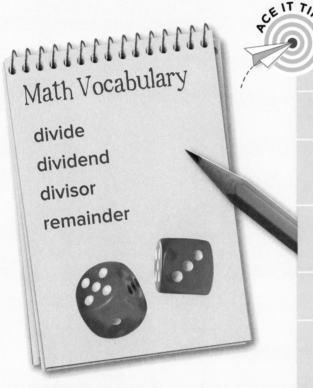

Math Vocabulary

divide

dividend

divisor

remainder

ACE IT TIME!

	yes	no
Did you underline the question in the word problem?	○	○
Did you circle the numbers or number words?	○	○
Did you box the supporting details or information needed to solve the problem?	○	○
Did you draw a picture or a graphic organizer and write a math sentence to show your thinking?	○	○
Did you label your numbers and your picture?	○	○
Did you explain your thinking and use math vocabulary words in your explanation?	○	○

MATH ON THE MOVE

Roll the dice! Create a four-digit dividend by rolling the dice four times. Roll the dice two more times to create a two-digit divisor. Divide using whichever strategy you feel most comfortable with. The next time you play, try a different strategy!

Interpreting Remainders

UNPACK THE STANDARD
You will interpret the remainders of division problems.

LEARN IT: A remainder can mean different things in different division problems. It all depends on what question the problem asks you to solve, and what the remainder actually represents.

Example: Carmen volunteered to make brownies for the fifth-grade celebration. There are 104 students in the fifth grade at her school. Each box of brownie mix makes 16 brownies.

WATCH OUT! Your answer will be different depending on the question!

Use only the quotient as the answer; drop the remainder.

How many WHOLE boxes of brownie mix will Carmen use?

To find the answer, you need to know how many equal groups of 16 go into 104, or $104 \div 16$.

think! The remainder 8 is only part of a whole group of 16, because 8 < 16.

$$16 \overline{)104} \quad 6 \text{ r}8$$

If $104 \div 16 = 6 \text{ r}8$, this means there are 6 equal groups of 16 with 8 left over. Carmen will use 6 whole boxes of brownies. The answer is the quotient only.

Add 1 to the quotient.

How many boxes of brownie mix will Carmen use to make brownies for everyone?

think! You don't want to leave anyone out, so you will use another box of brownie mix!

$$16 \overline{)104} \quad 6 \text{ r}8$$

Because there is a remainder, she will also use part of another box of brownie mix. Carmen will use 7 boxes of brownie mix to make enough brownies for everyone. You add 1 to the quotient.

Write the remainder as a fraction.

Ask yourself: Can she use part of a box? Yes! Carmen will use $6\frac{8}{16}$, or $6\frac{1}{2}$ boxes of mix.

$$16 \overline{)104} \quad 6 \text{ r}8$$

Write the remainder as a fraction. Use the remainder as the numerator, and the divisor as the dividend.

$$\frac{8}{16} = \frac{1}{2}$$ **Remember to simplify!**

Use only the remainder as the answer.

Carmen only has enough money to buy 6 boxes of brownies. How many students will not get brownies? Ask yourself: How many brownies did she need to make from the 7th box? She needs 8 brownies out of the 16, so 8 students will not get brownies. You used the remainder as the answer.

Standard: CCSS.Math.Content.5.NBT.B.6, 5.NF.B.3

PRACTICE: Now you try

Solve. Remember to pay attention to the question!

1. The fourth and fifth graders at Frandel Park Elementary are going on a field trip. There are 339 students. The principal decided to rent minivans to transport the students. Each minivan can hold 7 students.
   a. How many minivans will the school need to transport all of the students?
   b. One minivan will not be full. How many students will be in that minivan?

2. This summer, the Hutton family is having their family reunion. There are 237 family members going. They decided to rent cottages on the beach. Each cottage will hold 19 family members.
   a. How many cottages will be full?
   b. How many family members will be in the cottage that is not full?

The Apple School District wants to send all fifth-grade students on a class trip to New York City, also known as "The Big Apple." There are 2,467 fifth graders. They will be traveling in buses that hold 55 students. How many buses will be needed to take all of the students? How do you need to interpret the remainder? Show your work and explain your thinking on a piece of paper.

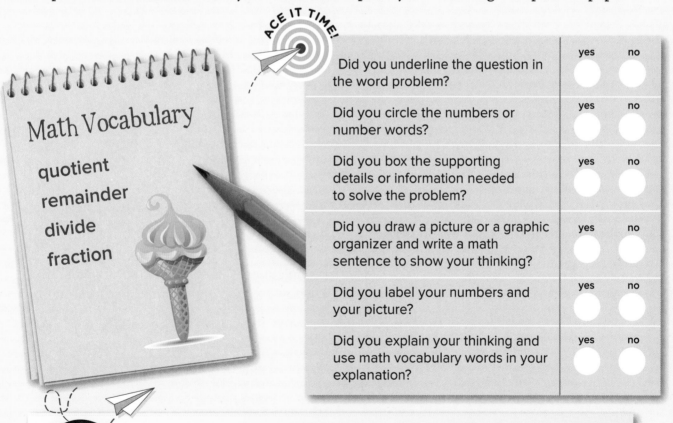

ACE IT TIME!

Math Vocabulary

quotient
remainder
divide
fraction

	yes	no
Did you underline the question in the word problem?	○	○
Did you circle the numbers or number words?	○	○
Did you box the supporting details or information needed to solve the problem?	○	○
Did you draw a picture or a graphic organizer and write a math sentence to show your thinking?	○	○
Did you label your numbers and your picture?	○	○
Did you explain your thinking and use math vocabulary words in your explanation?	○	○

MATH ON THE MOVE

Imagine you are hosting a party. Make a guest list of all the family and friends you want to invite. Then plan snacks you would like to have. How many boxes of your favorite snacks would you need to buy?

REVIEW

Congratulations! You've finished the lessons for this unit. This means you've learned about dividing with one-digit and two-digit divisors. You've learned how to divide using different strategies such as the area model, partial quotients, and the standard algorithm. You've also learned how to interpret remainders.

Now it's time to prove your skills with division. Solve the problems below! Use all of the methods you have learned.

Activity Section 1: One-Digit Divisors

Fill in the boxes to solve the following problems.

1. Kareem's soccer league has $264 to buy new soccer balls. Each ball costs $8. How many balls can they buy?	**2.** Mr. Yen pays $2 for each song he uploads to his laptop. He has spent $134 this year on songs. How many songs did he buy?
3. A factory produces 2,814 earbuds in 6 hours. How many earbuds does it produce in 1 hour?	**4.** The Bay Bridge High School's math department has a budget of $1,045 to buy calculators. If each calculator costs $5, how many can the math department buy?

Standards: CCSS.Math.Content.5.NBT.B.6, NF.B.3

Activity Section 2: Two-Digit Divisors

Fill in the boxes to solve the following problems.

1. $14\overline{)3{,}710}$	2. $36\overline{)7{,}812}$	3. $28\overline{)5{,}936}$
4. $56\overline{)4{,}567}$	5. $18\overline{)6{,}741}$	6. $25\overline{)3{,}100}$

7. The Oak County school district has $1,680 for scholarships. The money was awarded equally to 12 students. How much money did each student receive?

8. Samir has taken 2,032 pictures on his smartphone. His phone can show 16 pictures on the screen at one time. How many screens of 16 would Samir need to view in order to see all 2,032 pictures?

Activity Section 3: Interpreting Remainders

Use what you have learned about interpreting remainders to solve. Use your preferred method to divide, and show your work!

1. Mrs. Connolly is buying pencils for the students in her art class. She needs to order 1,267 pencils. The pencils come in cases of 55. How many cases should she order to have enough pencils for her students?

2. Luisa is playing a video game. She has earned 550 coins. She spends all of her coins buying new characters that cost 50 coins each. How many characters did she buy, and how many coins does she have left over?

3. The Science Club at your school is making balloon rockets. Mrs. Johns has 198 feet of string to share with the 36 members of the club. How many feet of string will each member receive?

4. Field trip! How many buses will the Sunny Hill Elementary School need for a field trip to the Kids' Discovery Center if each bus holds 42 people, and there are 115 fifth graders plus 5 teachers?

Standards: CCSS.Math.Content.5.NBT.B.6, NF.B.3

UNDERSTAND

Understand the meaning of what you have learned and apply your knowledge.

There are several methods you can use to solve a division problem. Try each method. Which method do you prefer and why?

Activity Section

Four students were asked to divide 2,430 by 15. Their work is listed below. Identify which method each student used. Which method do you prefer and why? Explain.

Timothy's way

```
        162
   15 ) 2,430
       -15
         93
       - 90
         30
       - 30
          0
```

Chris's way

```
              15
      100 | 1,500
       50 |   750
       10 |   150
        2 |    30    50 + 10 + 2 = 162
      100+
```

Lori's way

```
   15 ) 2,430
      -1,500      100
        930
      - 150       10
        780
      - 150       10
        630
      - 150       10
        480
      - 150       10
        330
      - 150       10
        180
      - 150       10
         30
      -  30        2
          0
                  162
```

Wendy's way

```
   15 ) 2,430
      -1,500      100
        930
      - 750        50
        180
      - 150        10
         30
      -  30         2
          0
                  162
```

DISCOVER

Discover how you can apply the information you have learned.

Activity Section

Keisha has a 115-inch piece of rope she is going to use for an art project. She plans to cut the rope into 12-inch pieces. She says that she will have 10 equal pieces. Is she correct? Explain why or why not.

Standards: CCSS.Math.Content.5.NF.B.3; CCSS.Math.Practice.MP1, MP2, MP3, MP4, MP6, MP7

CORE Adding and Subtracting Decimals Concepts

Place Value in Decimals

UNPACK THE STANDARD
You will read and write decimals up to the thousandths place.

LEARN IT: Remember that you count with base-ten numbers. Remember also how place value changes by powers of ten in whole numbers. Decimals use place value rules, too.

The base ten blocks (or a **hundreds grid**) model can help.

Example:

This column is $\frac{1}{10}$ of the whole. You can also write this as 0.1 or one-tenth.

How many blocks make a column? Because one block is $\frac{1}{10}$ of a column, it is $\frac{1}{100}$ of the whole. You can also write this as one hundredth or 0.01.

Imagine splitting the block into ten equal pieces. Those pieces would be $\frac{1}{1,000}$ of the whole, which is written as 0.001 or one thousandth.

Think of a **decimal place value chart.**

Example: Take a look at the value of 365.432 in the place value chart:

Hundreds 100	Tens 10	Ones 1	Tenths 0.1	Hundredths 0.01	Thousandths 0.001
3	6	5	4	3	2
3×100	6×10	5×1	$4 \times \frac{1}{10}$	$3 \times \frac{1}{100}$	$2 \times \frac{1}{1000}$

You can write the decimal 365.432 in **expanded form** as an expression:

Example: 365.432 can be written as the following expression:

$3 \times 100 + 6 \times 10 + 5 \times 1 + 4 \times (\frac{1}{10}) + 3 \times (\frac{1}{100}) + 2 \times (\frac{1}{1000})$.

In word form, you say, "Three hundred sixty-five and four hundred thirty-two thousandths."

think! Remember: The decimal point is read as "and" because you are adding a whole number and a fractional part (or a decimal).

PRACTICE: Now you try

Write the value of the underlined digit. Then, tell if it is in the tenths, hundredths, or thousandths place.

1. 23.5<u>8</u>7

2. 1.70<u>8</u>

Write the decimals in expanded form.

3. 44.444

4. 714.619

Write the decimals in word form.

5. 1.25

6. 12.406

Write the decimals in number form.

7. Twenty and sixteen hundredths

8. Four hundred seventy-two and nine hundred twenty-three thousandths

Bailey thinks the decimal 23.365 is written as "twenty-three and three hundred sixty-five hundredths." Jack thinks it is "twenty-three and three hundred sixty-five thousandths." Who do you think is correct and why? What error was made? Show your work and explain your thinking on a piece of paper.

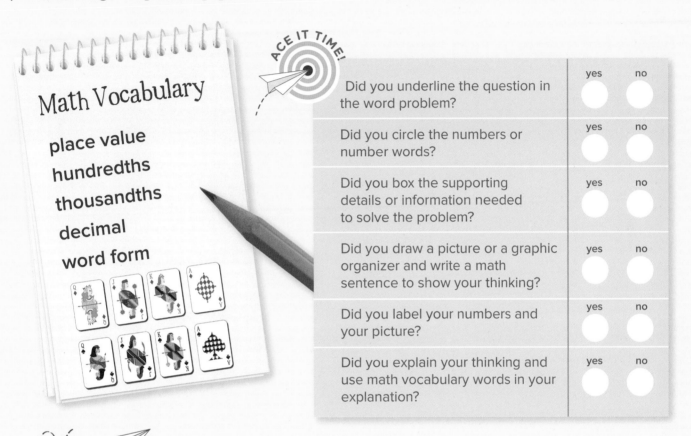

Math Vocabulary

place value
hundredths
thousandths
decimal
word form

ACE IT TIME!

	yes	no
Did you underline the question in the word problem?	○	○
Did you circle the numbers or number words?	○	○
Did you box the supporting details or information needed to solve the problem?	○	○
Did you draw a picture or a graphic organizer and write a math sentence to show your thinking?	○	○
Did you label your numbers and your picture?	○	○
Did you explain your thinking and use math vocabulary words in your explanation?	○	○

MATH ON THE MOVE

Practice reading and writing decimals to the thousandths place. Get a deck of cards. Separate out the aces and the cards with numbers 2–9 (aces equal 1). Deal four cards and write the numbers in sequence. Place a decimal between two of the numbers. Then write the decimal in expanded and word form. For example, if you dealt a 3, 5, 7, and 9, you could write 35.79. This is thirty-five and seventy-nine hundredths.

Comparing and Ordering Decimals

UNPACK THE STANDARD
You will compare the value of decimals and order decimals to the thousandths place.

LEARN IT: You can compare and order decimals the same way you compare and order whole numbers. Read decimals from left to right, or from greater to lesser place value. A chart can help you compare each digit and order them based on value.

Example: Which is greater: 1.457 or 1.475?

Ones	Tenths	Hundredths	Thousandths
1	4	5	7
1	4	7	5

Step 1:	Step 2:	Step 3:
Compare the digits in the ones place.	Compare the digits in the tenths place.	Compare the digits in the hundredths place.
1 = 1	4 = 4	7 > 5
The digits are equal. Move to the next place.	The digits are equal. Move to the next place.	So 1.475 > 1.457

REMEMBER TO LINE UP THE DECIMAL POINTS WHEN COMPARING NUMBERS!

PRACTICE: Now you try

Order these decimals from *least* to *greatest*. Record your answers in the space provided below.

1. 2.545, 25.450, 2.554	**2.** 21.550, 20.155, 21.551
3. 45.230, 45.233, 45.200	**4.** 0.411, 0.414, 0.114

Standard: CCSS.Math.Content.5.NBT.A.3.B

Order these decimals from *greatest* to *least*. Record your answers in the space provided below.

5. 51.151, 51.115, 51.551	**6.** 0.809, 0.089, 0.808
7. 0.002, 0.020, 0.200	**8.** 1.040, 1.400, 1.004

The average rainfall totals for the months of June through September in Tampa, Florida, are listed in the table. In which month did it rain the most? The least? How do you know? Use a place value chart to help you list the decimals in order from least to greatest. Show your work and explain your thinking on a piece of paper.

Average monthly rainfall in Tampa, FL (in inches)	
June	6.682
July	7.070
August	7.700
September	6.638

ACE IT TIME!

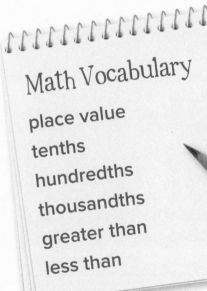

Math Vocabulary

place value

tenths

hundredths

thousandths

greater than

less than

	yes	no
Did you underline the question in the word problem?	○	○
Did you circle the numbers or number words?	○	○
Did you box the supporting details or information needed to solve the problem?	○	○
Did you draw a picture or a graphic organizer and write a math sentence to show your thinking?	○	○
Did you label your numbers and your picture?	○	○
Did you explain your thinking and use math vocabulary words in your explanation?	○	○

MATH ON THE MOVE

Roll the dice! Roll the dice to find three numbers. Use those numbers to create three different decimals, including a zero in each decimal. Then list the decimals in order from least to greatest. For example: You rolled a 1, 3, and 6. You could make the decimals 1.360, 1.036, and 1.630. Now list them in order from least to greatest.

Rounding Decimals

UNPACK THE STANDARD
You will round decimals up to a given place value.

LEARN IT: Rounding decimals uses the same strategy as rounding whole numbers. Think: "Five and above, give it a shove; four and below, let it go."

You can use a place value chart to help.

Example: Round **1.248** to the nearest hundredth.

Ones	Tenths	Hundredths	Thousandths
1	2	(4)	8

Step 1:	Step 2:	Step 3:	Step 4:
Circle the digit in the place value to which you want to round.	Underline the digit to the right of the place you are rounding.	If the underlined digit is less than 5, the circled digit stays the same. If the underlined digit is greater than or equal to 5, the circled digit increases by 1.	Drop the digits to the right of the circled digit.

1.248 rounded to the nearest hundredth is **1.25**

You can also round without a place value chart.

Example: Round **2.346** to the nearest whole number, tenths, and hundredths place.

Round to the nearest whole number:	Round to the nearest tenths place:	Round to the nearest hundredths place:
2 . 3 4 6	2 . 3 4 6	2 . 3 4 6
Think: 3 < 5, so the answer is 2.0.	Think: 4 < 5, so the answer is 2.3.	Think: 6 > 5, so the answer is 2.35.

Standard: CCSS.Math.Content.5.NBT.A.4

PRACTICE: Now you try

Round each decimal to the place that has the underlined digit.

1. 23.5<u>8</u>9 (Round to the tenths place)	2. 1.2<u>3</u>1 (Round to the hundredths place)
3. 0.0<u>6</u>1	4. 181.8<u>0</u>1
5. <u>9</u>.712	6. 0.00<u>7</u>
7. Jaxson's father fills up the family car with 18.1290 gallons of gas. How much gas is that, rounded to the nearest hundredth?	8. Pedro buys a DVD on sale for $16.99. How much money is that, rounded to the nearest dollar?

Explain what happens when you round 5.999 to the nearest tenth. Show your work and explain your thinking on a piece of paper.

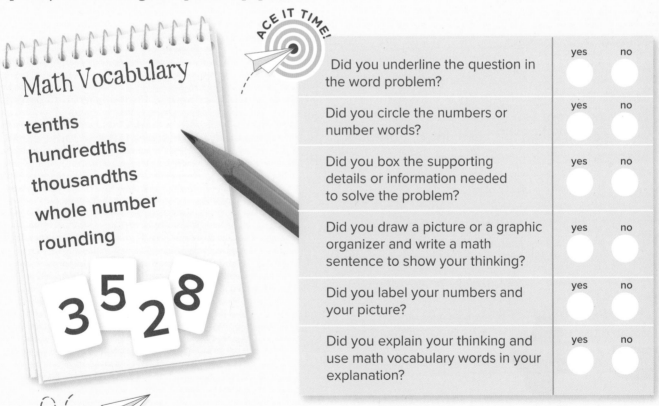

Math Vocabulary

tenths
hundredths
thousandths
whole number
rounding

3 5 2 8

ACE IT TIME!

	yes	no
Did you underline the question in the word problem?	◯	◯
Did you circle the numbers or number words?	◯	◯
Did you box the supporting details or information needed to solve the problem?	◯	◯
Did you draw a picture or a graphic organizer and write a math sentence to show your thinking?	◯	◯
Did you label your numbers and your picture?	◯	◯
Did you explain your thinking and use math vocabulary words in your explanation?	◯	◯

MATH ON THE MOVE

Flip the cards! Using number cards 1–9, flip four cards over to create a decimal to the thousandths place. Write the number down. First, round to the nearest whole number. Next, round it to the nearest tenth place, then to the nearest hundredth. For example, if you flip 3, 2, 5, and 8, you can create the number 3.258. Round it to the nearest whole number (3), tenth place (3.3), and then hundredths place (3.26).

Adding and Subtracting Decimals

UNPACK THE STANDARD
You will add and subtract decimals to the hundredths place.

LEARN IT: Adding and subtracting decimals is done the same way as adding and subtracting whole numbers. Just like you line up digits in the appropriate place value, you also line up the decimal points!

Example:

Add the following decimals: **4.22 + 7.71 = 11.93**	**Subtract** the following decimals: **15.35 − 2.84 = 12.51**

Step 1: Write the problem vertically and line up the decimal points.

$$
\begin{array}{r}
4.22 \\
+\ 7.71 \\
\hline
\end{array}
$$

Step 1: Write the problem vertically, and line up the decimal points.

$$
\begin{array}{r}
15.35 \\
-\ 2.84 \\
\hline
\end{array}
$$

Step 2: Add as you normally would with whole numbers. Start in the place all the way to the right (in this case, the hundredths place).

$$
\begin{array}{r}
4.22 \\
+\ 7.71 \\
\hline
11.93
\end{array}
$$

Step 2: Subtract as you normally would with whole numbers. Start in the place all the way to the right (in this case, the hundredths place.)

$$
\begin{array}{r}
\overset{4\ \ 13}{1\cancel{5}.\cancel{3}5} \\
-\ 2.84 \\
\hline
12.51
\end{array}
$$

think! Regroup as you would with whole numbers!

Standard: CCSS.Math.Content.5.NBT.B.7

PRACTICE: Now you try

Solve. Be sure to rewrite the problem vertically and line up the decimal points.

1. 45.36 + 2.77	**2.** 3.65 − 1.42
3. Angelo ran 1 mile in 8.38 minutes. His second mile was 8.75 minutes. How long did it take him to run these 2 miles?	**4.** Sammy's German Shepard weighs 73.20 pounds. His cousin's dog weighs 23.46 pounds less. How much does his cousin's dog weigh?

Mick has saved $14.35. Moe has saved $21.85. They want to combine their savings and buy a gift for their father that costs $40.00. How much more money do they need to save in order to buy the gift? Show your work and explain your thinking on a piece of paper.

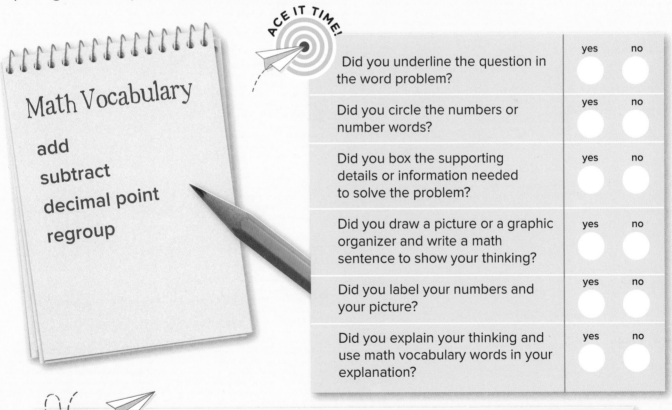

Math Vocabulary

add
subtract
decimal point
regroup

ACE IT TIME!

	yes	no
Did you underline the question in the word problem?	○	○
Did you circle the numbers or number words?	○	○
Did you box the supporting details or information needed to solve the problem?	○	○
Did you draw a picture or a graphic organizer and write a math sentence to show your thinking?	○	○
Did you label your numbers and your picture?	○	○
Did you explain your thinking and use math vocabulary words in your explanation?	○	○

MATH ON THE MOVE

Have a discussion with an adult or friend about real-life situations where you use decimals. Money is a great example! Can you find other places in your life where numbers are represented in decimal form?

REVIEW

Congratulations! You've finished the lessons for this unit. This means you've learned how to write decimals up to the thousandths place. You've practiced ordering decimals from least to greatest. You know how to round decimals to a given place value. You can even add and subtract decimals.

Now it's time to prove your skills with decimals. Solve the problems below! Use all of the methods you have learned.

Activity Section 1: Place Value in Decimals

Write each decimal in expanded and word form.

1. 0.568	**2.** 14.78
3. 400.25	**4.** 890.809
5. 708.02	**6.** 999.999

Activity Section 2: Comparing and Ordering Decimals

Compare the decimals. Write >, <, or = in each circle.

1. 2.003 ( ) 2.03	**2.** 14.144 ( ) 14.140
3. 58.8 ( ) 58.80	**4.** 9.09 ( ) 9.90
5. 67.76 ( ) 67.766	**6.** 81.56 ( ) 81.506

7. List the following big cats' weights in order from the heaviest to the lightest:
Ocelot: 25.35 lb; Canadian Lynx: 23.5 lb; Spanish Lynx: 29.25 lb; Bobcat: 29.03 lb

8. List the following plant heights in order from shortest to tallest:
4.222 cm, 4.202 cm, 4.002 cm, 4.220 cm

9. Jim and Randy challenged each other to a 25 yard race. Jim's time was 2.7 seconds, and Randy's time was 2.75 seconds. Who ran the fastest? How do you know?

Activity Section 3: Rounding Decimals

Round each decimal to the given place value.

1. Devon's batting average is 0.384. What is his batting average rounded to the nearest hundredth?

2. Hannah weighs 68.878 pounds. How much does she weigh rounded to the nearest whole number?

3. Quan is measuring a piece of wood. The wood measures 24.211 inches. What is 24.211 rounded to the nearest hundredth?

4. Micah measured 1.214 mL of liquid in his science beaker. How much liquid is that rounded to the nearest tenth?

5. Clara ran 3.702 miles on her run today. How many miles is that rounded to the nearest whole number?

Standards: CCSS.5.NBT.A.1, 5.NBT.A.3.A, 5.NBT.A.3.B, 5.NBT.A.4, 5.NBT.B.7

Activity Section 4: Adding and Subtracting Decimals

Solve the problems.

1. Megan and Conrad both had fevers. Megan's temperature was 101.7 degrees. Conrad's temperature was 1.5 degrees less. What was Conrad's temperature?

2. Henry ran 1.23 miles on Monday, 2.33 miles on Tuesday, and 2.83 miles on Wednesday. How many miles did he run on all 3 days?

3. Kim weighs 70.84 pounds. Dave weighs 74.21 pounds. How much more does Dave weigh than Kim?

4. The students of Rankin Elementary School had a fundraiser to raise money for their school's technology fund. They made $3,874.00 in October and $5,220.50 in May. How much money did the students raise in all? Their goal was to raise $10,000. How close were they to reaching their goal?

UNDERSTAND

Understand the meaning of what you have learned and apply your knowledge.

A strong understanding of place value is needed when comparing decimals. You should be comfortable comparing decimals based on the place value of each digit.

Activity Section

Place the digits 0, 3, 7, and 8 in each row of the table to create four decimals that are in order from least to greatest. The first one is done for you. *Hint:* Use all 4 digits in each row.

Ones	Tenths	Hundredths	Thousandths
0	3	7	8

Explain how you got your answer in the space below. What other decimals can you make with these digits? List them in order from least to greatest.

Standards: CCSS.Math.Content.5.NBT.A.3.B; CCSS.Math.Practice.MP1, MP2, MP3, MP4, MP5, MP6, MP7

DISCOVER

Activity Section

Which of the following decimals round to 4.5 when rounded to the nearest tenth? Explain how you know.

4.34	4.53	4.48
4.452	4.59	4.550

Can you think of more decimals which would round to 4.5 when rounded to the nearest tenth? List them below.

CORE Multiplying and Dividing Decimals Concepts

Multiplication Patterns with Decimals

UNPACK THE STANDARD
You will explain changes in the number of zeroes or the placement of decimal points when multiplying by tens.

LEARN IT: Multiplying a number by 10 changes it by one place value. Multiply 5×10 and you get 50. Multiply 10×10 and you get 100. The same changes happen with decimals. You can use patterns and powers of 10 to figure out where to place the decimal point after multiplying.

Try multiplying 3.14 by powers of 10. Follow the pattern below.
What do you notice?

Exponent:	Equation:	Decimal Point Placement:
0	$10^0 \times 3.14 = 3.14$	0 places to the right
1	$10^1 \times 3.14 = 31.4$	1 place to the right
2	$10^2 \times 3.14 = 314$	2 places to the right
3	$10^3 \times 3.14 = 3,140$	3 places to the right

Try multiplying 4,259 by decimals. Follow the pattern below.
What do you notice?

Decimal:	Equation:	Decimal Point Placement:
1	$1 \times 4,259 = 4,259$	0 places to the left
0.1	$0.1 \times 4,259 = 425.9$	1 place to the left
0.01	$0.01 \times 4,259 = 42.59$	2 places to the left
0.001	$0.001 \times 4,259 = 4.259$	3 places to the left

 Standards: CCSS.Math.Content.5.NBT.A.3.A, 5.NBT.B.7

PRACTICE: Now you try

Multiply the decimals.

1. $1 \times 7.15 =$ _____	**2.** $13.45 \times 10^0 =$ _____	**3.** $1 \times 6{,}124 =$ _____
$10 \times 7.15 =$ _____	$13.45 \times 10^1 =$ _____	$0.1 \times 6{,}124 =$ _____
$100 \times 7.15 =$ _____	$13.45 \times 10^2 =$ _____	$0.01 \times 6{,}124 =$ _____
$1{,}000 \times 7.15 =$ _____	$13.45 \times 10^3 =$ _____	$0.001 \times 6{,}124 =$ _____

Kendra and her friends are making necklaces to sell at their school's pep rally. They need to make 1,000 necklaces. Each necklace uses 1.55 feet of cord. Kendra did the math and figured out they need 1,055 feet of cord to make enough necklaces. Is she correct? Why or why not? Show your work and explain your thinking on a piece of paper.

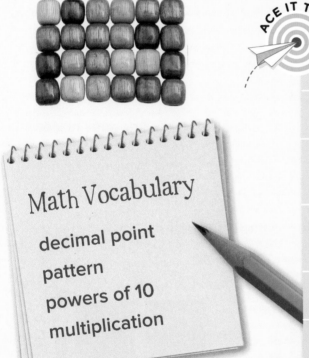

Math Vocabulary

decimal point

pattern

powers of 10

multiplication

ACE IT TIME!

	yes	no
Did you underline the question in the word problem?	○	○
Did you circle the numbers or number words?	○	○
Did you box the supporting details or information needed to solve the problem?	○	○
Did you draw a picture or a graphic organizer and write a math sentence to show your thinking?	○	○
Did you label your numbers and your picture?	○	○
Did you explain your thinking and use math vocabulary words in your explanation?	○	○

MATH ON THE MOVE

Left or right? Ask an adult or friend to play a game with you. Give your partner a decimal and a number to multiply by. Ask him or her if the decimal will move left or right. For example, you could give your partner 6.5 times 100. He or she would say the decimal point moves right, as follows: 6.5 x 100 = 650. Switch places and have your partner ask you, "Left or right?"

Multiplying Decimals and Whole Numbers

UNPACK THE STANDARD
You will multiply decimals to the hundredths place by whole numbers.

LEARN IT: Multiplying decimals follows the same rules as multiplying whole numbers. Use what you already know and apply the same strategies and methods.

Example: Solve 3 × 4.15.

Multiply as you would with whole numbers, then add the decimal point to the product.

Step 1:	Step 2:	Step 3:	Step 4:
Multiply the hundredths.	Multiply the tenths.	Multiply the ones.	How many decimal places are there? Count the decimal places in multiplied numbers. The product should have the same number of decimal places.

Step 1:

$$\begin{array}{r} 1 \\ 4.15 \\ \times \quad 3 \\ \hline 0\,5 \end{array}$$

Step 2:

$$\begin{array}{r} 1 \\ 4.15 \\ \times \quad 3 \\ \hline 4\,5 \end{array}$$

Step 3:

$$\begin{array}{r} 4.15 \\ \times \quad 3 \\ \hline 12\,4\,5 \end{array}$$

Step 4:

$$\begin{array}{rl} 4.15 & \text{2 decimal places} \\ \times \quad 3 & \longrightarrow \text{+ 0 decimal places} \\ \hline 12.45 & \longrightarrow \text{2 decimal places} \end{array}$$

You can also show decimal multiplication using base-ten blocks.
Draw 4.15 three times. Count the total, as shown below.

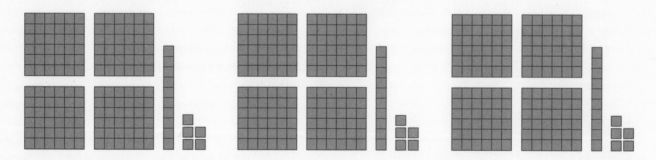

Add them together and you have 12 ones, 4 tenths, and 5 hundredths.

PRACTICE: Now you try

Multiply the following decimals and whole numbers.

1. 4.31 × 7 =	**2.** 8 × 2.35 =
3. 6 × 2.13 =	**4.** 5 × 1.24 =

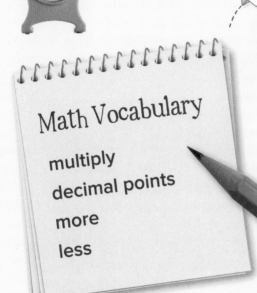

One pound of grapes costs $2.99 at the grocery store. Jeanine buys 3 pounds. Mark bought 2 pounds of grapes for $3.49 per pound at the farmer's market. Who spent less? How much less did he or she spend on grapes? Show your work and explain your thinking on a piece of paper.

ACE IT TIME!

	yes	no
Did you underline the question in the word problem?	○	○
Did you circle the numbers or number words?	○	○
Did you box the supporting details or information needed to solve the problem?	○	○
Did you draw a picture or a graphic organizer and write a math sentence to show your thinking?	○	○
Did you label your numbers and your picture?	○	○
Did you explain your thinking and use math vocabulary words in your explanation?	○	○

Math Vocabulary

multiply
decimal points
more
less

Use number cards 1–9. Flip four cards over to create a multiplication problem with a decimal and a whole number. For example, 1, 2, 5, and 6 could make the problem 12.5 × 6. Solve. Next, use those same numbers to create two other decimals. For example, you could create 0.125 and 1.25. Multiply each decimal by 6. Discuss how the product changes based on the decimal point placement.

Multiplying Decimals

UNPACK THE STANDARD
You will multiply decimals to the hundredths place by other decimals.

LEARN IT: Multiplying two decimals together is just like multiplying a decimal by a whole number. There will just be more decimal places in the answer because there are more decimal places to count! Remember that decimals represent parts of a whole. When you multiply them together, you are finding a part of a part.

Example: Solve 0.8 × 0.3.

You can solve 8 tenths × 3 tenths using a hundredths grid model. In a hundredths grid, each box represents one hundredth (0.01).

Step 1: Shade in 0.8 vertically.

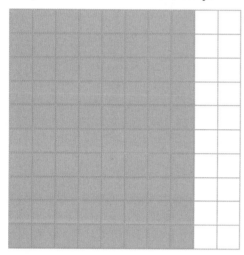

think! 0.24 is less than 0.8 and 0.3 because you are finding a part of a part! Will the product always be less than the factors? Look at 2.8 × 1.3 = 3.64. What do you notice about the decimal parts of the numbers?

Step 2: Shade in 0.3 horizontally.

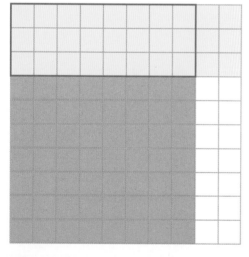

Step 3: Draw a box around the part that is shaded twice. In this diagram, 24 of the 100 boxes are shaded twice. This is $\frac{24}{100}$, or 0.24.

0.8 × 0.3 = 0.24

You can also solve using the standard algorithm. Place the correct decimal point in the end product!

0.7	1 decimal place
× 0.4	+ 1 decimal place
0.28	2 decimal places

Hint: Multiply as you normally would with whole numbers, and add the decimal point at the end!

PRACTICE: Now you try

Multiply the following decimals using any chosen method.

1. $1.5 \times 0.9 =$	**2.** $3.6 \times 4.2 =$
3. $5.2 \times 7.3 =$	**4.** $4.06 \times 7.4 =$
5. Stefan participates in a triathlon. It takes him 2.25 hours to complete the race. It takes his friend 1.5 times as long. How long does it take his friend to complete the race?	**6.** Cora spent $8.50 last month on music downloads. Talia spent 2.5 times as much as Cora on her downloads. How much did Talia spend?

Pele and Taka both solve the multiplication problem 4.5×0.4. Pele says the answer is 0.18, and Taka says the answer is 1.8. Who is correct and how do you know? Show your work and explain your thinking on a piece of paper.

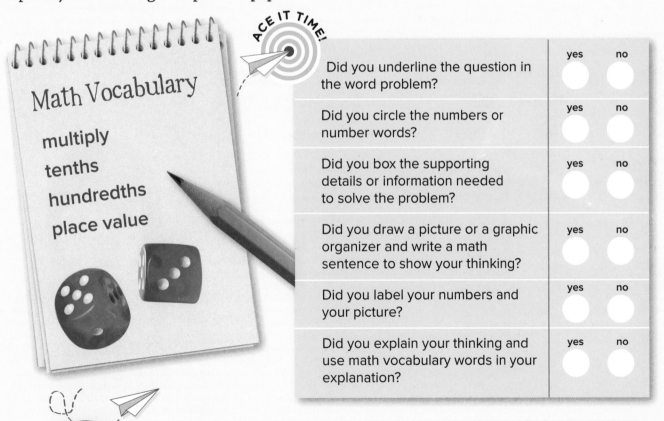

Math Vocabulary

multiply
tenths
hundredths
place value

ACE IT TIME!

	yes	no
Did you underline the question in the word problem?	○	○
Did you circle the numbers or number words?	○	○
Did you box the supporting details or information needed to solve the problem?	○	○
Did you draw a picture or a graphic organizer and write a math sentence to show your thinking?	○	○
Did you label your numbers and your picture?	○	○
Did you explain your thinking and use math vocabulary words in your explanation?	○	○

MATH ON THE MOVE

Roll the dice! Roll a die 4 times to create 2 decimals to the tenths place. For example, 2, 6, 3, 4 could make 2.6 and 3.4. Multiply the two decimals together.

Division Patterns with Decimals

UNPACK THE STANDARD
You will explain changes in the number of zeroes or the placement of decimal points when dividing by tens.

LEARN IT: Use your knowledge of place value and basic multiplication facts to multiply larger numbers with the standard algorithm, or method, of multiplication.

Divide 12.3 by powers of 10. You can use exponents to determine how the decimal point moves.

Exponent:	Equation:	Decimal Point Placement:
0	$12.3 \div 10^0 = 12.3$	0 places to the left
1	$12.3 \div 10^1 = 1.23$	1 place to the left
2	$12.3 \div 10^2 = 0.123$	2 places to the left

Divide 15.6 by multiples of 10. You can also use place value patterns.

Power of 10:	Equation:	Decimal Point Placement:
1	$15.6 \div 1 = 15.6$	0 places to the left
10	$15.6 \div 10 = 1.56$	1 place to the left
100	$15.6 \div 100 = 0.156$	2 places to the left

Standards: CCSS.Math.Content.5.NBT.A.3.A, 5.NBT.B.7

PRACTICE: Now you try

Find the quotients. Be sure to place the decimal point in the correct spot!

1. $242 \div 1 =$ _____

$242 \div 10 =$ _____

$242 \div 100 =$ _____

$242 \div 1{,}000 =$ _____

2. $38 \div 10^0 =$ _____

$38 \div 10^1 =$ _____

$38 \div 10^2 =$ _____

$38 \div 10^3 =$ _____

3. $146 \div 1 =$ _____

$146 \div 10 =$ _____

$146 \div 100 =$ _____

$146 \div 1{,}000 =$ _____

4. $11 \div 10^0 =$ _____

$11 \div 10^1 =$ _____

$11 \div 10^2 =$ _____

$11 \div 10^3 =$ _____

Ella thinks $15 \div 10^1$ is equal to the product of 15×0.1. Is she correct? Why or why not? Show your work and explain your thinking on a separate piece of paper.

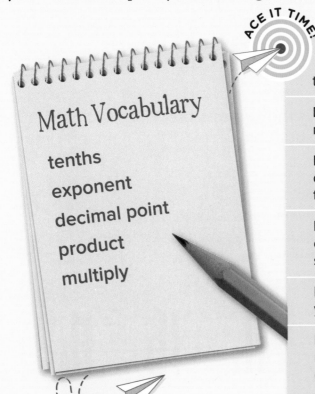

ACE IT TIME!

Math Vocabulary

tenths

exponent

decimal point

product

multiply

	yes	no
Did you underline the question in the word problem?	○	○
Did you circle the numbers or number words?	○	○
Did you box the supporting details or information needed to solve the problem?	○	○
Did you draw a picture or a graphic organizer and write a math sentence to show your thinking?	○	○
Did you label your numbers and your picture?	○	○
Did you explain your thinking and use math vocabulary words in your explanation?	○	○

MATH ON THE MOVE

Compare multiplying and dividing by powers of 10. How are they different? Why are they so similar?

Dividing Decimals and Whole Numbers

UNPACK THE STANDARD
You will divide decimals to the hundredths place by whole numbers.

LEARN IT: Dividing decimals can be done the same way as dividing whole numbers. Use similar methods. Make sure to put the decimal point in the quotient!

Example: Solve 1.25 ÷ 5.

Divide as you normally would with whole numbers. Add the decimal point to the quotient.

Step 1:	Step 2:
Divide without the decimal point.	Replace the decimal point in the dividend. Put it in the same spot in the quotient.
$$\begin{array}{r} 2\,5 \\ 5\,\overline{)1\,2\,5} \\ -\underline{1\,0}\downarrow \\ 2\,5 \\ -\underline{2\,5} \\ 0 \end{array}$$	$$\begin{array}{r} .2\,5 \\ 5\,\overline{)1.2\,5} \\ -\underline{1\,0}\downarrow \\ 2\,5 \\ -\underline{2\,5} \\ 0 \end{array}$$

Divide using base-ten blocks. To divide by 5 is the same as breaking a number into five equal groups. You might have to break bigger blocks (or whole numbers) into tenths, and tenths into hundredths.

Step 1:	Step 2:
Show 1.25 with base ten blocks or a drawing to represent.	Break apart the flat (or 1 whole) into longs (or 10 tenths). Divide the longs into 5 equal groups. Break apart the remaining 2 longs into blocks (or 20 hundredths). You should have 25 blocks (0.25) to divide into five groups.
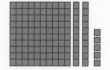	 

Step 3:

Notice how each group has 0 flats (wholes), 2 longs (tenths), and 5 blocks (hundredths).

$$1.25 \div 5 = 0.25$$

PRACTICE: Now you try

Divide the following decimals and whole numbers.

1. 2.24 ÷ 4 =	**2.** 4.14 ÷ 3 =
3. 3.24 ÷ 9 =	**4.** 7.50 ÷ 6 =

Leah and her 3 friends want to go bowling. It will cost $50.60 for all of them to go. How much will it cost for each person? Show your work and explain your thinking on a piece of paper.

ACE IT TIME!

Math Vocabulary

divide

decimal points

place value

2 3 8 9

	yes	no
Did you underline the question in the word problem?	○	○
Did you circle the numbers or number words?	○	○
Did you box the supporting details or information needed to solve the problem?	○	○
Did you draw a picture or a graphic organizer and write a math sentence to show your thinking?	○	○
Did you label your numbers and your picture?	○	○
Did you explain your thinking and use math vocabulary words in your explanation?	○	○

MATH ON THE MOVE

Use number cards 1–9. Flip four cards over to create a division problem with a decimal and a whole number. For example, 2, 3, 8, and 9 could make the problem 3.98 ÷ 2. Make sure your numbers are divisible. You can check the divisibility rules at *www.mathsisfun.com/divisibility-rules.html*. Solve your problem and play again!

Dividing Decimals

UNPACK THE STANDARD

You will divide decimals to the hundredths place by other decimals.

LEARN IT: When you divide a decimal by a decimal, use what you have learned about dividing a decimal by a whole number. You can also use your knowledge of decimal place value.

Example: Solve 1.75 ÷ 0.25.

You can use a decimal base-ten model.

Step 1:	Step 2:
Shade the decimal model to show 1.75.	Break apart the model into groups of 25 hundredths (or 0.25).
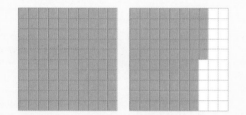	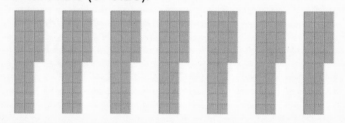

The model now shows 7 groups of 0.25. So 1.75 ÷ 0.25 = 7.

You can also use the standard algorithm of division and your knowledge of powers of 10. Move the decimal point in the divisor to make it a whole number. Then move the same number of places in the dividend. Place the decimal point above in the quotient.

Step 1:	Step 2:	Step 3:
Multiply by a power of 10 to make the divisor a whole number. 0.25 × 100 = **25**	Multiply the dividend by the same power of 10. 1.75 × 100 = **175.0**	Now divide with the "new" numbers. $\begin{array}{r} 7.0 \\ 25\overline{)175.0} \\ -175 \\ \hline 0 \end{array}$ **think!** 1.75 ÷ 0.25 = 7

Standard: CCSS.Math.Content.5.NBT.B.7

PRACTICE: Now you try

Divide the following decimals.

1. 5.6 ÷ 0.8 =	**2.** 1.75 ÷ 0.5 =
3. 0.18 ÷ 0.9 =	**4.** 0.64 ÷ 0.08 =

Calvin wants to break $2.00 into dimes. How many dimes will he have? (*Hint:* How do you use decimals to show the amount of money in a dime?) Show your work and explain your thinking on a piece of paper.

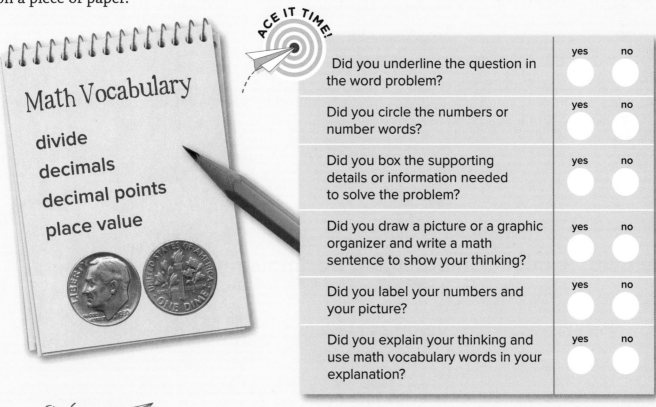

Math Vocabulary

divide
decimals
decimal points
place value

ACE IT TIME!

	yes	no
Did you underline the question in the word problem?		
Did you circle the numbers or number words?		
Did you box the supporting details or information needed to solve the problem?		
Did you draw a picture or a graphic organizer and write a math sentence to show your thinking?		
Did you label your numbers and your picture?		
Did you explain your thinking and use math vocabulary words in your explanation?		

MATH ON THE MOVE

Compare multiplying and dividing decimals. How are they the same? How are they different? Look for examples in real life where you would divide decimals.

REVIEW

Stop and think about what you have learned.

Congratulations! You've finished the lessons for this unit. This means you've learned how decimal points move when you multiply and divide by tens. You've practiced multiplying and dividing decimals by whole numbers. You can even multiply and divide decimals by other decimals. You can use models, and you can use the standard algorithm.

Now it's time to prove your skills with decimals. Solve the problems below! Use all of the methods you have learned.

Activity Section 1: Multiplication Patterns with Decimals

Solve the following problems.

1. $1 \times 2.6 =$ _____ $10 \times 2.6 =$ _____ $100 \times 2.6 =$ _____ $1{,}000 \times 2.6 =$ _____	**2.** $1 \times 56 =$ _____ $0.1 \times 56 =$ _____ $0.01 \times 56 =$ _____	**3.** $10^0 \times 23.88 =$ _____ $10^1 \times 23.88 =$ _____ $10^2 \times 23.88 =$ _____ $10^3 \times 23.88 =$ _____
4. Meara is making team spirit ribbons for a pep rally. The length of each ribbon is 4.45 inches. If she needs to make 1,000 ribbons, how much ribbon does she need in all? 		

Activity Section 2: Multiplying Decimals and Whole Numbers

Solve the following problems.

1. $2.45 \times 8 =$	**2.** $47 \times 4.7 =$	**3.** $286 \times 0.95 =$
4. A car travels 60.5 miles per hour. How many miles will it have traveled in 12 hours?		

Standards: CCSS.Math.Content.5.NBT.A.3.A, 5.NBT.B.7

Activity Section 3: Multiplying Decimals

Solve the following problems.

1. $2.2 \times 3.8 =$	**2.** $37.8 \times 0.25 =$	**3.** $5.40 \times 0.4 =$
4. Brennan measured a plant in his backyard that was 3.2 feet tall. Six weeks later, the plant was 1.5 times as tall. How tall was the plant after the 6 weeks?		

Activity Section 4: Division Patterns with Decimals

Solve the following problems.

| **1.** $556 \div 1 =$ _____

 $556 \div 10 =$ _____

 $556 \div 100 =$ _____

 $556 \div 1{,}000 =$ _____ | **2.** $88.8 \div 1 =$ _____

 $88.8 \div 10 =$ _____

 $88.8 \div 100 =$ _____ | **3.** $405 \div 10^0 =$ _____

 $405 \div 10^1 =$ _____

 $405 \div 10^2 =$ _____

 $405 \div 10^3 =$ _____ |
| **4.** The local bakery uses 425 pounds of flour to make 100 loaves of bread. How many pounds of flour are used for 1 loaf of bread? | | |

Activity Section 5: Dividing Decimals and Whole Numbers

Solve the following problems.

1. 6.40 ÷ 8 =	**2.** 3.24 ÷ 4 =	**3.** 80.5 ÷ 5 =
4. Mr. O'Grady paid $42.80 for tickets to the fair for his son, James, and his 3 friends. How much did each ticket cost?		

Activity Section 6: Dividing Decimals

Solve the following problems.

1. 8.10 ÷ 0.9 =	**2.** 56.0 ÷ 0.07 =	**3.** 16.2 ÷ 0.2 =
4. Ashanti went to the market and bought 3.6 pounds of strawberries to share with her family. If each family member receives 0.4 pounds of strawberries, how many family members is she sharing with?		

Standards: CCSS.Math.Content.5.NBT.A.3.A, 5.NBT.B.7

UNDERSTAND

Understand the meaning of what you have learned and apply your knowledge.

You have learned about the place value of decimals. You have also learned how to multiply and divide with decimals. Use what you know to solve this multi-step problem. You'll have to choose when to divide, multiply, add, or subtract.

Activity Section

Jennie spent $8.60 at the store. Frankie spent 4 times as much as Jennie. Craig spent $5.88 more than Frankie. How much money did Frankie and Craig spend? Show your work and explain how you got your answer.

DISCOVER

Activity Section

Elise spent $27.79 on 3 books and 4 notebooks. Each book cost $6.99, and the total sales tax was $1.82. If each notebook cost an equal amount, how much did each notebook cost?

Standards: CCSS.Math.Content.5.NBT.B.7; CCSS.Math.Practice.MP1, MP2, MP4, MP6, MP7

CORE Adding and Subtracting Fractions Concepts

Adding and Subtracting Fractions with Unlike Denominators

UNPACK THE STANDARD
You will use models to add and subtract fractions with unlike denominators.

LEARN IT: Models are a good way to show addition and subtraction of fractions. One simple model can help you add $\frac{1}{2}$ to $\frac{1}{4}$.

Example: Solve: $\frac{1}{2} + \frac{1}{4}$.

You can add using fraction strips.
Cut out the fraction strips on page 183.

Notice how the fraction strips $\frac{1}{2}$ and $\frac{2}{4}$ take up the same amount of space. They are equal. You can add $\frac{2}{4}$ and $\frac{1}{4}$ because they have the same denominator.
$\frac{2}{4} + \frac{1}{4} = \frac{3}{4}$

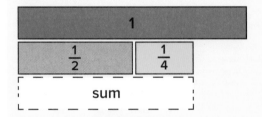

1 Whole					
$\frac{1}{2}$			$\frac{1}{2}$		
$\frac{1}{3}$		$\frac{1}{3}$		$\frac{1}{3}$	
$\frac{1}{4}$	$\frac{1}{4}$	$\frac{1}{4}$	$\frac{1}{4}$		
$\frac{1}{5}$	$\frac{1}{5}$	$\frac{1}{5}$	$\frac{1}{5}$	$\frac{1}{5}$	
$\frac{1}{6}$	$\frac{1}{6}$	$\frac{1}{6}$	$\frac{1}{6}$	$\frac{1}{6}$	$\frac{1}{6}$
$\frac{1}{8}$ $\frac{1}{8}$ $\frac{1}{8}$ $\frac{1}{8}$ $\frac{1}{8}$ $\frac{1}{8}$ $\frac{1}{8}$ $\frac{1}{8}$					
$\frac{1}{10}$ $\frac{1}{10}$ $\frac{1}{10}$ $\frac{1}{10}$ $\frac{1}{10}$ $\frac{1}{10}$ $\frac{1}{10}$ $\frac{1}{10}$ $\frac{1}{10}$ $\frac{1}{10}$					
$\frac{1}{12}$ $\frac{1}{12}$ $\frac{1}{12}$ $\frac{1}{12}$ $\frac{1}{12}$ $\frac{1}{12}$ $\frac{1}{12}$ $\frac{1}{12}$ $\frac{1}{12}$ $\frac{1}{12}$ $\frac{1}{12}$ $\frac{1}{12}$					

You can add using an area model.

Step 1:

Draw two rectangles of the same size. Separate them into parts to show fractions. The first rectangle shows halves. The second rectangle shows fourths.

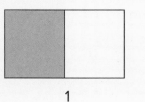 +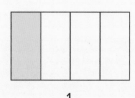

$\frac{1}{2}$ + $\frac{1}{4}$

Step 2:

Divide each rectangle into new parts. How many parts? Use the denominator of the other fraction. Divide the rectangle showing halves ($\frac{1}{2}$) into four new parts ($\frac{1}{4}$). Divide the rectangle showing fourths ($\frac{1}{4}$) into two new parts ($\frac{1}{2}$).

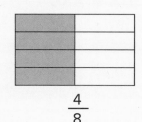 +

$\frac{4}{8}$ + $\frac{2}{8}$

Step 3:

The rectangles show $\frac{4}{8}$ and $\frac{2}{8}$. You can add them because they have the same denominator. $\frac{4}{8} + \frac{2}{8} = \frac{6}{8}$. Remember to simplify! $\frac{6}{8} = \frac{3}{4}$.

The same models can be used to subtract fractions with unlike denominators.

Example: Solve $\frac{5}{6} - \frac{1}{3}$.

Step 1: Show $\frac{5}{6}$. You can use the fraction strips on page 183!

Step 2: Show $\frac{1}{3}$ under the $\frac{5}{6}$.

Step 3: Find which strips fit exactly in the empty spot. Three $\frac{1}{6}$ strips fit, so $\frac{5}{6} - \frac{1}{3} = \frac{3}{6}$.

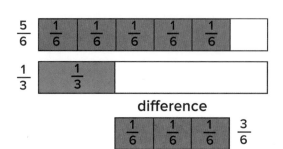

Standard: CCSS.Math.Content.5.NF.A.2

PRACTICE: Now you try

Add or subtract the following fractions.

1. $\frac{1}{10} + \frac{2}{8} =$	**2.** $\frac{1}{2} + \frac{3}{10} =$
3. $\frac{5}{6} - \frac{1}{2} =$	**4.** $\frac{2}{3} - \frac{1}{6} =$

Mario used $\frac{1}{3}$ cup of almonds and $\frac{1}{4}$ cup of raisins to make a trail mix. After he mixed those 2 ingredients, he gave $\frac{1}{2}$ cup of the mix to his brother. How much trail mix did he have left? Show your work and explain your thinking on a piece of paper.

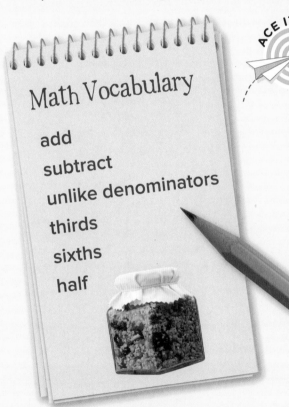

Math Vocabulary

add

subtract

unlike denominators

thirds

sixths

half

ACE IT TIME!

	yes	no
Did you underline the question in the word problem?	○	○
Did you circle the numbers or number words?	○	○
Did you box the supporting details or information needed to solve the problem?	○	○
Did you draw a picture or a graphic organizer and write a math sentence to show your thinking?	○	○
Did you label your numbers and your picture?	○	○
Did you explain your thinking and use math vocabulary words in your explanation?	○	○

MATH ON THE MOVE Write or tell a story that involves adding or subtracting fractions with unlike denominators. Be sure to include a solution!

The Common Denominator

UNPACK THE STANDARD
You will add and subtract fractions with unlike denominators by changing those fractions to a common denominator.

LEARN IT: You can use models to add and subtract fractions. You can also use _common denominators._ When fractions have the same number on the bottom, this is called a common denominator. Changing unlike numbers to similar numbers makes the addition and subtraction easy.

Example: Solve $\frac{3}{4} + \frac{2}{12}$ by finding the common denominator. To find the common denominator, first list the multiples.

Step 1:	Step 2:
List the multiples of each denominator. 4: 4, 8, ⃝12, 16, 20, 24 . . . 12: ⃝12, 24, 36, 48 . . . Look at the multiples that are the same. Circle the lowest one. Use this as the new bottom number. **think!** Why don't you use 24 as the denominator? Is it possible?	Change the top numbers by the same amount as the bottom numbers. Remember, multiples are used in multiplication! $\frac{3}{4} = \frac{9}{12}$ $\frac{2}{12} = \frac{2}{12}$ **think!** $4 \times ? = 12$. You multiply by 3 to get 12. Multiply the top number by the same amount.

Step 3:

Add the fractions with like denominators: $\frac{9}{12} + \frac{2}{12} = \frac{11}{12}$

(Remember, when adding and subtracting fractions, you only add or subtract the top number. The bottom number stays the same.)

You can also multiply the bottoms of the fractions together. However, you will not always get the _lowest_ (or _least_) common denominator. You may have to simplify your final answer!

Step 1:	Step 2:
Multiply the denominators. $\frac{3}{4} + \frac{2}{12}$ ($4 \times 12 = 48$) The product (48) is a multiple of both numbers.	Change the top numbers by the same amount. $\frac{3 \times 12}{4 \times 12} = \frac{36}{48}$

Standard: CCSS.Math.Content.5.NF.A.1

Step 3:

Add the fractions. $$\frac{36}{48} + \frac{8}{48} = \frac{44}{48}$$	You can simplify $\frac{44}{48}$ because both the numbers are multiples of 2. You can tell because they are both even. Divide each by 2 until you can't simplify any more: $$\frac{44}{48} = \frac{22}{24} = \frac{11}{12}$$ The answer in simplest form is $\frac{11}{12}$.

PRACTICE: Now you try

Add or subtract the following fractions.

1. $\frac{3}{8} + \frac{1}{4} =$	**2.** $\frac{3}{4} - \frac{1}{2} =$	**3.** $\frac{1}{2} - \frac{3}{9} =$

Jackson is making friendship bracelets. He starts with $\frac{4}{5}$ meter of twine and uses $\frac{3}{10}$ meter of twine on each bracelet. How much twine is left after one bracelet? Using subtraction, figure out how many bracelets Jackson can make. Show your work and explain your thinkng on a piece of paper.

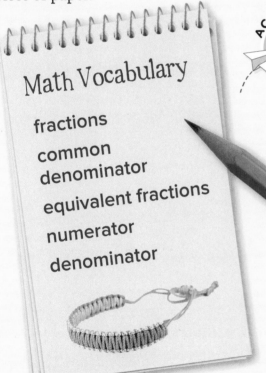

Math Vocabulary

fractions

common denominator

equivalent fractions

numerator

denominator

ACE IT TIME!

	yes	no
Did you underline the question in the word problem?	○	○
Did you circle the numbers or number words?	○	○
Did you box the supporting details or information needed to solve the problem?	○	○
Did you draw a picture or a graphic organizer and write a math sentence to show your thinking?	○	○
Did you label your numbers and your picture?	○	○
Did you explain your thinking and use math vocabulary words in your explanation?	○	○

MATH ON THE MOVE

Write or talk about how you solve $\frac{2}{9} + \frac{3}{12}$ by finding the common denominator. Why is it easier to use the least common denominator?

Adding and Subtracting Mixed Numbers

UNPACK THE STANDARD
You will use common denominators to add and subtract mixed numbers.

LEARN IT: A *mixed number* is a number that contains a whole number and a fraction. You can add and subtract mixed numbers like you do regular fractions. Make sure each fraction has a common denominator.

Example: Solve $2\frac{1}{3} + 1\frac{2}{6}$.

Step 1:	Step 2:	Step 3:
Change the fractions using the common denominator. $$2\frac{1}{3} = 2\frac{2}{6}$$ $$1\frac{2}{6} = 1\frac{2}{6}$$	Add the fractions first. Then, add the whole numbers: $$\begin{array}{r} 2\frac{2}{6} \\ + 1\frac{2}{6} \\ \hline + 3\frac{4}{6} \end{array}$$	Simplify the fraction. $$3\frac{4 \div 2}{6 \div 2} = 3\frac{2}{3}$$

Follow these steps for subtracting mixed numbers as well!

think! What happens if you get an improper fraction when adding? Example: $2\frac{1}{3} + 1\frac{5}{6} = 3\frac{7}{6}$. The number $\frac{7}{6}$ is improper because it is more than 1 ($\frac{6}{6}$). How do you simplify? *Hint: You carry the 1!* $3\frac{7}{6} = 4\frac{1}{6}$

You can also use a number line.
Example: Solve $3\frac{1}{2} + 1\frac{7}{8}$.

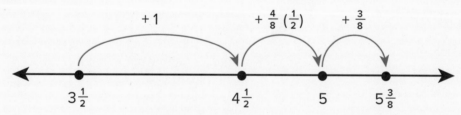

Step 1:	Step 2:	Step 3:
Draw a number line starting at the first mixed number ($3\frac{1}{2}$).	Use "easy jumps" to jump a total of $1\frac{7}{8}$ down the line. Try 1 whole and $\frac{1}{2}$. Because you are working in eighths, write $\frac{1}{2}$ with the common denominator 8.	Add the remaining $\frac{3}{8}$. $$3\frac{1}{2} + 1\frac{7}{8} = 5\frac{3}{8}$$

Standard: CCSS.Math.Content.5.NF.A.1

PRACTICE: Now you try

Add or subtract the following fractions.

1. $5\frac{2}{3} + 7\frac{3}{12} =$	**2.** $2\frac{3}{5} - 1\frac{1}{2} =$
3. $1\frac{2}{5} + 2\frac{3}{15} =$	**4.** $8\frac{3}{4} - 6\frac{1}{2} =$

Zea and Gabe walked in their town's Fourth of July parade. They both walked $2\frac{3}{8}$ miles during the parade. Afterward, Zea walked $\frac{3}{4}$ mile home, and Gabe walked $\frac{7}{8}$ mile home. How many miles did each of them walk that day? Zea thinks she walked more than Gabe. Do you agree with her? Who walked more that day, and how much more did that person walk? Show your work and explain your thinking on a piece of paper.

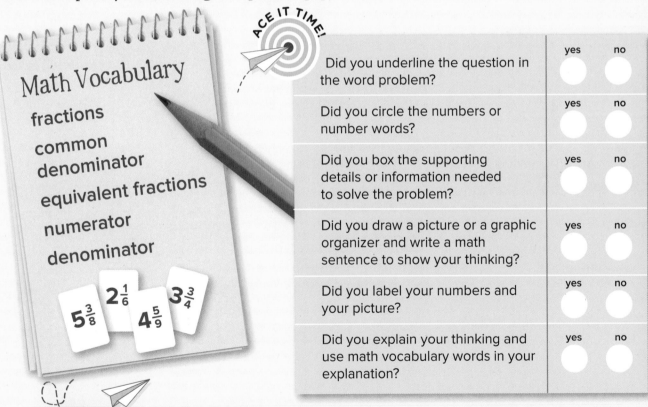

Math Vocabulary

fractions

common denominator

equivalent fractions

numerator

denominator

$5\frac{3}{8}$ $2\frac{1}{6}$ $4\frac{5}{9}$ $3\frac{3}{4}$

ACE IT TIME!

	yes	no
Did you underline the question in the word problem?	○	○
Did you circle the numbers or number words?	○	○
Did you box the supporting details or information needed to solve the problem?	○	○
Did you draw a picture or a graphic organizer and write a math sentence to show your thinking?	○	○
Did you label your numbers and your picture?	○	○
Did you explain your thinking and use math vocabulary words in your explanation?	○	○

MATH ON THE MOVE

Write mixed numbers on index cards. Shuffle the cards and flip two over. Decide if you want to add or subtract the mixed numbers. Find a common denominator and solve.

Subtracting Mixed Numbers with Regrouping

UNPACK THE STANDARD
You will use regrouping to subtract mixed numbers.

LEARN IT: Think about subtraction. What happens when you subtract a larger number from a smaller one? Think about subtracting 19 from 315. The 5 in the ones place is smaller than the 9. You have to regroup. You borrow from the tens place. The same thing happens in mixed numbers.

$$\begin{array}{r} {\scriptstyle 2\ 10\ 15} \\ \cancel{3}\cancel{1}5 \\ -\quad 19 \\ \hline 296 \end{array}$$

Example: Solve $5\frac{1}{3} - 1\frac{4}{6}$.

Step 1:	Step 2:	Step 3:
Change the fractions using the common denominator. $5\frac{1}{3} = 5\frac{2}{6}$ $1\frac{4}{6} = 1\frac{4}{6}$	Subtract the fractions first. Then, subtract the whole numbers: $\begin{array}{r}5\frac{2}{6}\\-1\frac{4}{6}\\\hline\end{array}$ **think!** We're working in sixths. How do you write 1 whole as a fraction? $\frac{6}{6} = 1$ $\frac{6}{6} + \frac{2}{6} = \frac{8}{6}$	Regroup. Finish subtracting. $\begin{array}{r}{\scriptstyle 4\ 8}\\5\frac{\cancel{2}}{6}\\-1\frac{4}{6}\\\hline 3\frac{4}{6} = 3\frac{2}{3}\end{array}$ Remember to simplify!

You can also solve by using improper fractions.
Example: Solve $5\frac{1}{3} - 1\frac{4}{6}$.

Step 1:	Step 2:	Step 3:
Change to common denominators. $5\frac{1}{3} = 5\frac{2}{6}$ $1\frac{4}{6} = 1\frac{4}{6}$	Convert each mixed number to an improper fraction (a fraction greater than one). $5\frac{2}{6} = \frac{32}{6}$ **think!** $\frac{6}{6} \times 5 = \frac{30}{6}$ $1\frac{4}{6} = \frac{10}{6}$	Subtract. $\begin{array}{r}\frac{32}{6}\\-\frac{10}{6}\\\hline\frac{22}{6}\end{array}$
Step 4: Convert the improper fraction back into mixed number form. $$\frac{22}{6} = 3\frac{4}{6} = 3\frac{2}{3}$$		

Standard: CCSS.Math.Content.5.NF.A.2

PRACTICE: Now you try

Subtract these mixed numbers.

1. $5\frac{1}{2} - 3\frac{4}{5} =$	**2.** $12\frac{1}{9} - 7\frac{1}{3} =$
3. $8 - 1\frac{4}{6} =$ **think!** You can also write the top number as $8\frac{0}{6}$. Regroup!	**4.** $9\frac{1}{4} - 3\frac{2}{3} =$

Carla incorrectly solved the problem $8\frac{2}{4} - 2\frac{4}{6}$ and got the answer $5\frac{8}{12}$. Where did she make an error? Show your work and explain your thinking on a piece of paper.

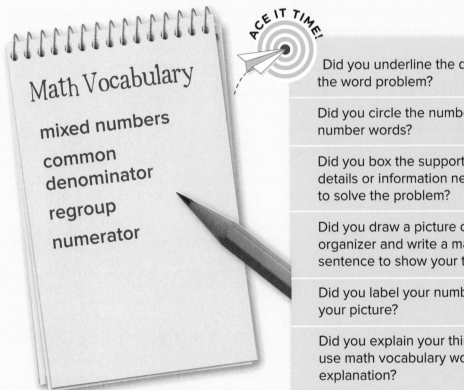

Math Vocabulary

- mixed numbers
- common denominator
- regroup
- numerator

ACE IT TIME!

	yes	no
Did you underline the question in the word problem?	○	○
Did you circle the numbers or number words?	○	○
Did you box the supporting details or information needed to solve the problem?	○	○
Did you draw a picture or a graphic organizer and write a math sentence to show your thinking?	○	○
Did you label your numbers and your picture?	○	○
Did you explain your thinking and use math vocabulary words in your explanation?	○	○

MATH ON THE MOVE

Find an adult or friend. Practice writing one whole as fractions. Tell your partner which fraction to write. If you tell your partner to write in fifths, he or she should write $\frac{5}{5}$. Then it's your partner's turn to tell you how to write one whole.

REVIEW

Congratulations! You've finished the lessons for this unit. This means you've learned how to add and subtract fractions with unlike denominators. You've used models, found common denominators, and learned how to add and subtract mixed numbers.

Now it's time to prove your skills with fractions. Solve the problems below! Use all of the methods you have learned.

Activity Section 1: Adding and Subtracting Fractions with Unlike Denominators

Solve the problems and answer the questions below.

1. $\frac{5}{8} + \frac{2}{4} =$	**2.** $\frac{3}{9} + \frac{5}{5} =$	**3.** $\frac{4}{9} + \frac{2}{3} =$
4. $\frac{2}{5} - \frac{1}{10} =$	**5.** $\frac{2}{3} - \frac{2}{6} =$	**6.** $\frac{4}{5} - \frac{1}{10} =$

7. Rylan has read $\frac{3}{4}$ of his book on his e-reader. Brad has read $\frac{1}{8}$ of his book. How much more has Rylan read than Brad?

8. Amir practices his guitar for $\frac{2}{4}$ of an hour at guitar lessons. When he gets home, he practices for another $\frac{2}{3}$ of an hour. How long did he practice playing his guitar in all? Bonus: How many minutes is that?

Activity Section 2: The Common Denominator

Rewrite the fractions with common denominators.

1. $\frac{3}{5}$, $\frac{4}{10}$

$\frac{3}{5} = \frac{\square}{\square}$ $\frac{4}{10} = \frac{\square}{\square}$

2. $\frac{3}{6}$, $\frac{4}{12}$

$\frac{3}{6} = \frac{\square}{\square}$ $\frac{4}{12} = \frac{\square}{\square}$

3. $\frac{8}{9}$, $\frac{2}{3}$

$\frac{8}{9} = \frac{\square}{\square}$ $\frac{2}{3} = \frac{\square}{\square}$

Solve using a common denominator.

4. $\frac{7}{9} + \frac{1}{3} =$

5. $\frac{3}{4} - \frac{3}{8} =$

6. $\frac{4}{6} + \frac{3}{5} =$

7. Shamar collected $\frac{3}{6}$ of a pound of paper at school to recycle. Liza collected $\frac{2}{8}$ of a pound. How many pounds of paper did they collect together?

8. Kristi had $\frac{4}{6}$ of a protein bar left. Her brother had $\frac{1}{3}$ of a bar left. How much more did Kristi have than her brother?

Activity Section 3: Adding and Subtracting Mixed Numbers

Solve the following problems.

1. Gunnar walked $2\frac{2}{8}$ miles for his school's walk-a-thon. Travis walked $3\frac{3}{4}$ miles. How many more miles did Travis walk than Gunnar?

2. At the recycling center, there were $6\frac{2}{3}$ pounds of crushed cans. There were $2\frac{1}{2}$ pounds of uncrushed cans. How many more pounds of cans were crushed than uncrushed?

3. Cole had $4\frac{3}{4}$ feet of rope to use to build a tire swing. His father gave him $8\frac{2}{3}$ feet of extra rope to build the swing. How much rope does he have to build the swing?

4. Annie has $4\frac{4}{6}$ feet of pink yarn to knit a scarf. She buys $6\frac{1}{2}$ feet of purple yarn. How much yarn does she have to knit her scarf?

5. Colton found a $6\frac{1}{2}$ foot piece of wood in his garage. He saws $1\frac{1}{3}$ feet off the board. How long is the piece of wood now?

6. Antonia uses $6\frac{3}{8}$ cups of orange juice and $3\frac{1}{4}$ cups of lemon-lime soda to make punch to share at the fifth-grade dance. How much punch will she have in all?

Standards: CCSS.Math.Content.5.NF.A.1, 5.NF.A.2

Activity Section 4: Subtracting Mixed Numbers with Regrouping

Solve. **Remember to regroup!**

1. $3\frac{2}{6} - 1\frac{4}{6} =$	**2.** $7\frac{2}{3} - 2\frac{5}{6} =$
3. $4\frac{3}{8} - 3\frac{1}{2} =$	**4.** $7\frac{1}{2} - 5\frac{4}{7} =$

5. Sydney had $12\frac{1}{2}$ inches of curling ribbon. She used $6\frac{2}{3}$ inches of ribbon to wrap a gift for her friend. How much ribbon was left?

UNDERSTAND

Understand the meaning of what you have learned and apply your knowledge.

You can apply your skills to add mixed numbers in a real-world setting. This problem will require you to master the art of this problem-solving, as well as master using a "guess and check" method.

Activity Section

Jorge is going on a camping trip. He has packed 4 bags of camping gear that weigh $7\frac{5}{8}$ lb, $8\frac{7}{8}$ lb, $15\frac{1}{2}$ lb, and $8\frac{1}{4}$ lb. He can only bring 25 pounds of gear. Which bags can he bring with him? He wants to bring as much gear as possible without exceeding the limit. Show your work and explain your reasoning in the space provided.

Standards: CCSS.Math.Content.5.NF.A.1; CCSS.Math.Practice.MP.1, MP.2, MP.3, MP.4, MP.6, MP.7, MP.8

DISCOVER

Discover how you can apply the information you have learned.

Activity Section

Cheyenne had a rain gauge in her backyard. She recorded the amount of rain over a 4-week period in July. She emptied the rain gauge at the end of each week to prepare for the next week's collection. Use the information in the table below to answer the following questions.

Week 1	$\frac{3}{4}$ in.
Week 2	$1\frac{2}{3}$ in.
Week 3	$2\frac{1}{2}$ in.
Week 4	$1\frac{1}{4}$ in.

1. How many inches did it rain in total during weeks 1 and 2?

2. How many inches did it rain in total during weeks 3 and 4?

3. How many inches did it rain in the whole month of July?

4. How much more did it rain in week 3 than in week 2?

5. How much more did it rain in week 4 than in week 1?

CORE Multiplying Fractions Concepts

Fractional Parts

UNPACK THE STANDARD
You will find fractional parts of whole numbers.

LEARN IT: A *fractional part* is part of a group. To find the fractional part, use models or multiplication and division.

Example: Solve $\frac{4}{5}$ of 20.

You can draw a model to solve.

Step 1:	Step 2:	Step 3:
Use shapes to show the group of 20.	Split the shapes into five equal groups, or fifths.	Count the shapes in four groups (four-fifths).
		$\frac{4}{5}$ of 20 = 16

You can multiply and divide to solve.

Step 1: Find $\frac{1}{5}$ of 20.	Step 2: Find $\frac{4}{5}$ of 20.
$20 \div 5 = 4$	$4 \times 4 = 16$
$\frac{1}{5}$ of 20 = 4	$\frac{4}{5}$ of 20 = 16
think! When you split 20 into 5 groups, what operation do you use?	**think!** If one-fifth of the group equals four, what operation do you use to find four-fifths?

Standard: CCSS.Math.Content.5.NF.B.4.A

PRACTICE: Now you try

Find the fractional parts.

1. Circle $\frac{3}{4}$ of 8. ●●●● ●●●● $\frac{3}{4}$ of 8 = _____	**2.** Circle $\frac{2}{3}$ of 12. ●●●●●● ●●●●●● $\frac{2}{3}$ of 12 = _____
3. $\frac{3}{8} \times 24 =$ _____	**4.** $\frac{4}{7} \times 21 =$ _____

The local animal shelter had 40 pets up for adoption. If $\frac{2}{5}$ of the pets were cats and $\frac{3}{5}$ were dogs, how many pets were cats? How many were dogs? Show your work and explain your thinking on a piece of paper.

ACE IT TIME!

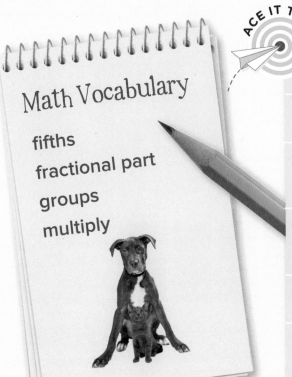

Math Vocabulary

fifths
fractional part
groups
multiply

	yes	no
Did you underline the question in the word problem?	○	○
Did you circle the numbers or number words?	○	○
Did you box the supporting details or information needed to solve the problem?	○	○
Did you draw a picture or a graphic organizer and write a math sentence to show your thinking?	○	○
Did you label your numbers and your picture?	○	○
Did you explain your thinking and use math vocabulary words in your explanation?	○	○

MATH ON THE MOVE

When do you find fractional amounts in the real world? Look for other examples in real-world situations and discuss with an adult or friend.

Making Sense of Fractions, Factors, and Products

UNPACK THE STANDARD
You will predict the size of a product compared to the size of its factors.

LEARN IT: Think about what you've learned about multiplying. Multiplying by a number greater than 1 gives you a larger product. Multiplying by a number less than 1 gives you a fractional part. You can predict the size of the product without actually multiplying the factors.

Example: $5 \times 1\frac{1}{5}$ is greater than 5. 5×1 is equal to 5. $5 \times \frac{1}{5}$ is less than 5.

5×1	$5 \times \frac{1}{5}$	$5 \times 1\frac{1}{5}$
When multiplying by 1, the product is **equal to** 5.	Is $\frac{1}{5}$ greater than 1? No. The product is **less than** 5.	Is $1\frac{1}{5}$ greater than 1? Read it aloud: one and one-fifth. Because $1\frac{1}{5}$ is greater than 1, the product is **greater than** 5.
think! Remember the Identity Property!	**think!** Multiplying by $\frac{1}{5}$ is the same as finding the fractional part. Can parts be greater than the whole?	**think!** Multiplying is a quick way of adding. Multiplying by $1\frac{1}{5}$ is the same as adding one 5 and a fractional part of 5. When you add, the sum is larger!

You can check your answers using a rectangle model.

5×1
The product will be equal to the 5 factor.
    SOLVE: $5 \times 1 = 5$
            $5 = 5$

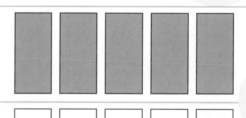

think! Imagine putting all the shaded boxes into one box. How many boxes would you fill up?

$5 \times \frac{1}{5}$
The product will be less than the 5 factor.
    SOLVE: $5 \times \frac{1}{5} = 1$
            $1 < 5$

$5 \times 1\frac{1}{5}$
The product will be greater than the 5 factor.
    SOLVE: $5 \times 1\frac{1}{5} = 6$
            $6 > 5$

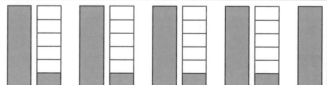

Standard: CCSS.Math.Content.5.NF.B.5

PRACTICE: Now you try

Fill in the blanks with greater than, less than, or equal to.

1. $\frac{7}{8} \times 1$ is _____ $\frac{7}{8}$	**2.** $\frac{5}{6} \times 2$ is _____ $\frac{5}{6}$
3. $3 \times \frac{4}{8}$ is _____ 3	**4.** $15 \times \frac{2}{3}$ is _____ 15
5. $\frac{5}{6} \times \frac{4}{4}$ is _____ $\frac{5}{6}$	**6.** $\frac{2}{8} \times 6$ is _____ $\frac{2}{8}$

Carlos thinks the product of $\frac{1}{4} \times \frac{2}{3}$ is greater than $\frac{1}{4}$. Emily thinks the product is less than $\frac{1}{4}$. Which of them is correct? Why? Show your work and explain your thinking on a piece of paper.

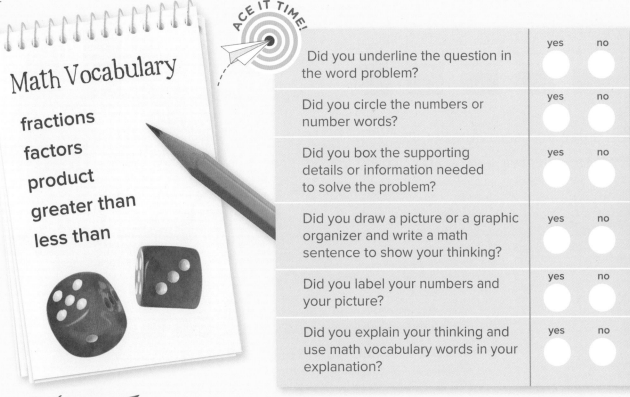

Math Vocabulary

fractions
factors
product
greater than
less than

ACE IT TIME!

	yes	no
Did you underline the question in the word problem?		
Did you circle the numbers or number words?		
Did you box the supporting details or information needed to solve the problem?		
Did you draw a picture or a graphic organizer and write a math sentence to show your thinking?		
Did you label your numbers and your picture?		
Did you explain your thinking and use math vocabulary words in your explanation?		

MATH ON THE MOVE

Using a regular set of dice, roll four times to create two fractions. Explain if the product of those factors would be less than, greater than, or equal to each of the factors. You can also use the dice to create a whole number to multiply with your fraction.

Multiplying Fractions and Whole Numbers

UNPACK THE STANDARD
You will multiply whole numbers by a fraction.

LEARN IT: There are many different ways to multiply a whole number by a fraction. Remember to check your work. Multiplying by a fraction means the product should be less than the whole number.

Example: Solve $5 \times \frac{3}{8}$.

You can draw a model to solve.

Step 1:	Step 2:
Draw 5 rectangles and split into eighths. Shade $\frac{3}{8}$ of each rectangle. 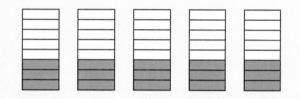	Rearrange the shaded pieces to fit as many whole rectangles as possible. Count the total. $5 \times \frac{3}{8} = 1\frac{7}{8}$ 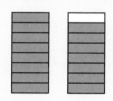

You can also use a number line.

Draw a number line starting at 0. Show 5 hops of $\frac{3}{8}$ each.

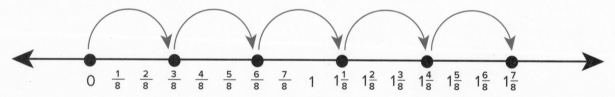

So, $5 \times \frac{3}{8} = 1\frac{7}{8}$

think! Remember the Commutative Property of Multiplication. $5 \times \frac{3}{8} = \frac{3}{8} \times 5$
Think of $5 \times \frac{3}{8}$ as "a $\frac{3}{8}$ fractional part of 5."
Think of $\frac{3}{8} \times 5$ as "$\frac{3}{8}$ five times."

Use the multiplication facts you know. Remember to simplify your fractions!

Step 1:	Step 2:
5 is a whole number, so you show it as $\frac{5}{1}$.	Multiply the numerators together, and multiply the denominators together. $$\frac{5}{1} \times \frac{3}{8} = \frac{15}{8} = 1\frac{7}{8}$$

Standard: CCSS.Math.Content.5.NF.B.5.B

PRACTICE: Now you try

Solve the problems. Write your answer in simplest form.

1. $\frac{2}{6} \times 6 =$	**2.** $4 \times \frac{3}{4} =$
3. $5 \times \frac{2}{6} =$	**4.** $\frac{2}{8} \times 3 =$
5. Leo lives $\frac{7}{8}$ miles from school. Shayne lives twice as far. How far from school does Shayne live?	**6.** Joy uploaded 8 new games to her smartphone. Her little sister has $\frac{3}{4}$ as many games. How many games does her sister have?

Maeko drew the model below for a problem. Write 2 problems that can be solved using this model. You should use a whole number multiplied by a fraction in your problems. Shade in the model to show how you'd solve. Show your work and explain your work on a piece of paper.

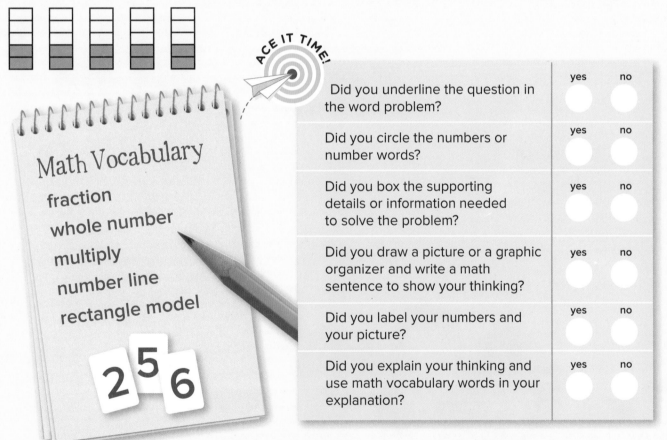

Math Vocabulary

fraction

whole number

multiply

number line

rectangle model

2 5 6

ACE IT TIME!

	yes	no
Did you underline the question in the word problem?	○	○
Did you circle the numbers or number words?	○	○
Did you box the supporting details or information needed to solve the problem?	○	○
Did you draw a picture or a graphic organizer and write a math sentence to show your thinking?	○	○
Did you label your numbers and your picture?	○	○
Did you explain your thinking and use math vocabulary words in your explanation?	○	○

MATH ON THE MOVE

Use number cards 1–9. Flip 3 cards over. Create a multiplication problem using one fraction. For example, if you flip a 2, 5, and 6, you can create the problem $2 \times \frac{5}{6}$. Solve.

Multiplying Fractions

UNPACK THE STANDARD
You will multiply a fraction by a fraction.

LEARN IT: Use an *area model* to multiply two fractions. Remember that the product should be less than the factors. Multiplying a fraction by a fraction is the same as finding a part of a part. Let's use the area model to multiply *mixed numbers*, or fractions with a whole number and a fractional part.

Example: Solve $\frac{3}{5} \times \frac{2}{3}$.

Step 1:

Draw a 5-by-3 rectangle to represent the denominators (fifths and thirds).

think! If you draw a 3 by 5 rectangle, will you get the same results? Remember the Commutative Property of Multiplication.

Step 2:
Shade in $\frac{2}{3}$ and $\frac{3}{5}$.

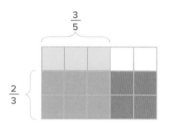

Step 3:

The product is the part that is shaded twice.

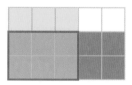

$$\frac{2}{3} \times \frac{3}{5} = \frac{6}{15} \text{ or } \frac{2}{5}$$

think! The numerator of the product (6) is equal to 2 x 3. The denominator (15) is equal to 3 x 5. Can you use basic multiplication to multiply fractions? Did you do this in a previous lesson?

Standard: CSS.Math.Content.5.NF.B.4.A

PRACTICE: Now you try

Find the products. Remember to simplify!

1. $\frac{1}{4} \times \frac{1}{2} =$	**2.** $\frac{3}{6} \times \frac{1}{3} =$
3. $\frac{4}{6} \times \frac{2}{4} =$	**4.** $\frac{3}{5} \times \frac{1}{3} =$
5. Three-fourths of the students in Mrs. Ramirez's class are girls. Five-sixths of those girls have brown eyes. Brown-eyed girls make up what fraction of the class?	**6.** Jordan measured the rain in her rain gauge at $\frac{3}{4}$ inch. The next day, $\frac{1}{3}$ of the water had evaporated from the rain gauge. How many inches of water had evaporated?

Jim orders a large cheese pizza. It comes with 12 slices. He eats $\frac{1}{3}$ of the slices. His brother Jon comes over and eats $\frac{1}{4}$ of the leftover slices. What fraction of the whole pizza does Jon eat? How many slices is that? Use an area model to help. *Hint:* How much of the pizza is left when Jon comes over? Show your work and explain your thinking on a piece of paper.

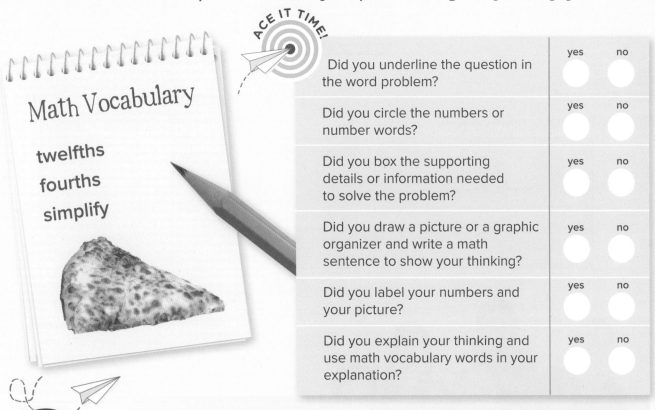

Math Vocabulary

twelfths

fourths

simplify

ACE IT TIME!

	yes	no
Did you underline the question in the word problem?	◯	◯
Did you circle the numbers or number words?	◯	◯
Did you box the supporting details or information needed to solve the problem?	◯	◯
Did you draw a picture or a graphic organizer and write a math sentence to show your thinking?	◯	◯
Did you label your numbers and your picture?	◯	◯
Did you explain your thinking and use math vocabulary words in your explanation?	◯	◯

MATH ON THE MOVE

Roll the dice four times to create a fraction multiplication problem. The highest numbers rolled will be the denominators. The other two numbers will be the numerators. For example, you roll 2, 4, 4, and 5. The denominators are 4 and 5. The numerators are 2 and 4. The problem to solve is $\frac{2}{4} \times \frac{4}{5}$.

Area and Mixed Numbers

UNPACK THE STANDARD
You will multiply mixed numbers by using an area model.

LEARN IT: Do you remember the formula for the area of a rectangle? (Area = length × width) The *area model* of multiplication uses that same formula. You can multiply to find the area of a rectangle with fractional side lengths.

Example: Solve $2\frac{3}{4} \times 1\frac{3}{5}$.

Step 1:	Step 2:	Step 3:
Separate each mixed number into a whole part and fractional part. $$2\frac{3}{4} = 2 + \frac{3}{4}$$ $$1\frac{3}{5} = 1 + \frac{3}{5}$$	Draw a rectangle to represent the problem.	Break the rectangle into pieces showing the numbers.

Step 4:	Step 5:
Find the area of each rectangle.	Add the fractional parts. $$2 + 1\frac{1}{5} + \frac{3}{4} + \frac{9}{20} = \frac{88}{20} = 4\frac{8}{20} = 4\frac{2}{5}$$

Step 4 areas:
- $1 \times 2 = 2$
- $1 \times \frac{3}{4} = \frac{3}{4}$
- $\frac{3}{5} \times 2 = 1\frac{1}{5}$
- $\frac{3}{5} \times \frac{3}{4} = \frac{9}{20}$

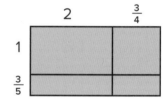

think! Use what you know about adding fractions with unlike denominators!

PRACTICE: Now you try

Find the products. Remember to simplify.

1. $1\frac{1}{4} \times 1\frac{1}{2} =$	**2.** $1\frac{2}{3} \times 1\frac{1}{3} =$
3. Kay's garden is $2\frac{2}{3}$ feet long by $2\frac{3}{4}$ feet wide. What is the area of her garden?	**4.** Your wall mirror is $1\frac{3}{4}$ feet long and $2\frac{1}{2}$ feet high. What is the area of the mirror?

Jonah's parents want to retile the entryway by their front door. The floor is $3\frac{1}{2}$ feet by $5\frac{3}{4}$ feet. What is the area of the floor they want to tile? Use a model to help you solve. Show your work and explain your thinking on a piece of paper.

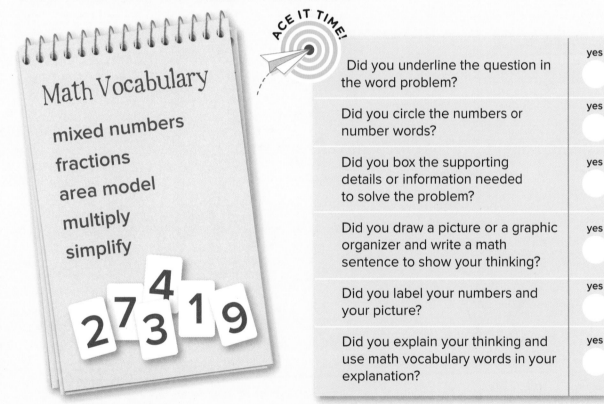

Math Vocabulary

mixed numbers

fractions

area model

multiply

simplify

ACE IT TIME!

	yes	no
Did you underline the question in the word problem?	○	○
Did you circle the numbers or number words?	○	○
Did you box the supporting details or information needed to solve the problem?	○	○
Did you draw a picture or a graphic organizer and write a math sentence to show your thinking?	○	○
Did you label your numbers and your picture?	○	○
Did you explain your thinking and use math vocabulary words in your explanation?	○	○

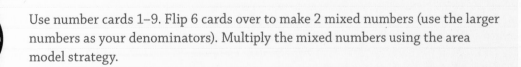

MATH ON THE MOVE

Use number cards 1–9. Flip 6 cards over to make 2 mixed numbers (use the larger numbers as your denominators). Multiply the mixed numbers using the area model strategy.

Multiplication with Mixed Numbers

UNPACK THE STANDARD
You will solve real-world problems that use fractions and mixed numbers.

LEARN IT: Identify which numbers you need to use. Decide whether to add, subtract, multiply, or divide. Remember that you multiply to find a fractional part.

Example: A park is $1\frac{1}{4}$ acres. One-third of the park has oak trees. How many acres of the park have oak trees? $1\frac{1}{4} \times \frac{1}{3} =$ _____ acres.

You can use a model to solve.

Step 1:	Step 2:
Draw two rectangles. Split them vertically into fourths. Shade $1\frac{1}{4}$. Split the rectangles horizontally into thirds. Shade one of the thirds. 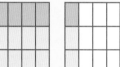	Count the parts that were shaded twice. $(\frac{4}{12} + \frac{1}{12} = \frac{5}{12})$ $$1\frac{1}{4} \times \frac{1}{3} = \frac{5}{12}$$

You can use improper fractions (fractions greater than 1).

Step 1:	Step 2:
Convert each mixed number into an improper fraction. $$1\frac{1}{4} = \frac{5}{4} \qquad \frac{5}{4} \times \frac{1}{3}$$ **think!** $1\frac{1}{4} = 1$ whole $+ \frac{1}{4}$. This is the same as $\frac{4}{4} + \frac{1}{4}$.	Multiply the improper fractions: $$\frac{5}{4} \times \frac{1}{3} = \frac{5}{12}$$

Use the Distributive Property.

Example:

$1\frac{1}{4} \times \frac{1}{3}$
$= (1 \times \frac{1}{3}) + (\frac{1}{4} \times \frac{1}{3})$
$= (\frac{1}{3}) + (\frac{1}{12})$
$= \frac{5}{12}$

think! Remember the Distributive Property from previous lessons! You can think of $1\frac{1}{4}$ as $(1 + \frac{1}{4})$. How else can you write $1\frac{1}{4} \times \frac{1}{3}$?

Standard: CCSS.Math.Content.5.NF.B.6

PRACTICE: Now you try

Solve the following problems.

1. Dimitri's puppy weighs $6\frac{5}{6}$ lbs. His sister's puppy weighs $\frac{3}{4}$ as much. How much does Dimitri's sister's puppy weigh?	**2.** Jada is making 16 friendship bracelets. Each bracelet uses $2\frac{1}{2}$ feet of cord. How much cord will she use?
3. Wendi lives $4\frac{3}{6}$ miles from school. Kevin lives $1\frac{1}{2}$ times as far away as Wendi. How many miles does Kevin live from school?	**4.** A fenced-in garden at the dog park is $3\frac{4}{5}$ feet long by $2\frac{1}{3}$ feet wide. How big is the garden?

You are making punch for a party. The recipe uses $5\frac{3}{4}$ cups of fruit juice. Using $1\frac{1}{2}$ times the ingredients in the recipe makes the perfect amount of punch for the party. How much fruit juice will you need? Show your work and explain your thinking on a piece of paper.

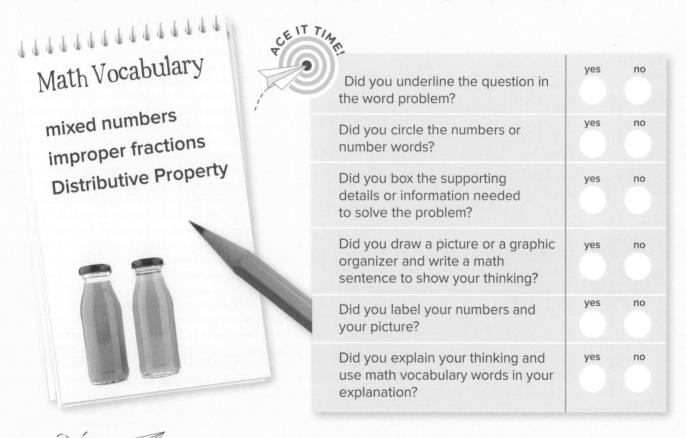

Math Vocabulary

mixed numbers
improper fractions
Distributive Property

ACE IT TIME!

	yes	no
Did you underline the question in the word problem?	○	○
Did you circle the numbers or number words?	○	○
Did you box the supporting details or information needed to solve the problem?	○	○
Did you draw a picture or a graphic organizer and write a math sentence to show your thinking?	○	○
Did you label your numbers and your picture?	○	○
Did you explain your thinking and use math vocabulary words in your explanation?	○	○

MATH ON THE MOVE

Talk with an adult or friend. Explain how multiplying a mixed number by a whole number is similar to multiplying two mixed numbers.

Stop and think about what you have learned.

Congratulations! You've finished the lessons for this unit. This means you've learned how to find fractional parts of whole numbers. You can multiply fractions by fractions. You can use many methods to multiply mixed numbers. You can even predict whether a product will be greater than or less than its products.

Now it's time to prove your skills with fractions and mixed numbers. Solve the problems below. Use all the methods you have learned.

Activity Section 1: Fractional Parts

Solve the following problems.

1. $\frac{3}{5}$ of 25 = _____

2. $\frac{7}{8} \times 32$ = _____

3. $\frac{4}{9}$ of 27 = _____

4. There are 24 flowers in the garden. Two-sixths of the flowers are red. The rest are yellow. How many of the flowers are red? How many of them are yellow?

5. Jeremiah downloaded 36 applications to his tablet. One-third of them are for school, and the rest are for fun! How many of his apps are for school? How many are for fun?

Standards: CCSS.Math.Content.5.NF.B.4.A, 5.NF.B.4.B, 5.NF.B.5.A, 5.NF.B.5.B, 5.NF.B.6

Activity Section 2: Making Sense of Fractions, Factors, and Products

Solve the following problems by writing *greater than, less than,* or *equal to.*

1. $\frac{3}{4}$ × 18 is _____ 18.	**2.** $\frac{3}{2}$ × 12 is _____ 12.
3. $\frac{1}{4}$ × $\frac{2}{5}$ is _____ $\frac{2}{5}$.	**4.** 4 × $\frac{5}{6}$ is _____ $\frac{5}{6}$.

5. Ryan is planting two flower beds. The first flower bed is 4 feet long and $\frac{7}{8}$ foot wide. The second flower bed is 4 feet long and $\frac{4}{6}$ foot wide. Compare the areas of the flower beds. Which flower bed is larger? Are they larger or smaller than 4 square feet?

6. Maia runs a concession stand at the local minor league baseball field. She is comparing last year's sales with the sales she has made so far this year. Last year, she sold $8,450 worth of food. It is now August, and she has made $\frac{3}{4}$ times as many sales as last year. Write an expression to describe the amount of money Maia has made so far this year. Has Maia sold more or less than last year?

Activity Section 3: Multiplying Fractions and Whole Numbers

Solve the following problems.

1. Use a rectangle model to show $\frac{4}{6}$ × 6.

2. Use a number line to show $\frac{1}{5}$ × 3.	**3.** Use both a number line and a rectangle model to show 4 × $\frac{2}{3}$.

4. Kris is wrapping gifts. He has 3 rolls of wrapping paper. If he uses $\frac{1}{4}$ of each roll, how many rolls of wrapping paper will he use in all?

5. Ellie is filling a jar with differently colored layers of sand. She has six 1 lb bags of colored sand and uses $\frac{2}{3}$ of each bag. How many pounds of sand will she use for the whole project?

Activity Section 4: Multiplying Fractions

Solve the following problems.

1. $\frac{4}{8} \times \frac{3}{4} =$	**2.** $\frac{3}{9} \times \frac{1}{2} =$	**3.** $\frac{3}{7} \times \frac{2}{3} =$

4. Zoe is making zucchini muffins. The recipe calls for $\frac{3}{4}$ cup of shredded zucchini. She only has $\frac{1}{3}$ of this amount. How many cups of shredded zucchini does Zoe have?

5. Mrs. Sian bought $\frac{6}{8}$ lbs. of sliced turkey at the deli. She used $\frac{2}{3}$ of the turkey to make sandwiches for her children. How many pounds of turkey did she use to make the sandwiches?

Activity Section 5: Area and Mixed Numbers

Solve the following problems.

1. $2\frac{1}{4} \times 1\frac{1}{4} =$

2	$\frac{1}{4}$
1	
$\frac{1}{4}$	

2. $4\frac{5}{6} \times 2\frac{2}{3} =$

4	$\frac{5}{6}$
2	
$\frac{2}{3}$	

3. Mr. Roberts' backyard has a fenced-in section for his dog. The section is $3\frac{1}{4}$ meters long and $2\frac{2}{8}$ meters wide. What is the area of the fenced-in section?

Standards: CCSS.Math.Content.5.NF.B.4.A, 5.NF.B.4.B, 5.NF.B.5.A, 5.NF.B.5.B, 5.NF.B.6

Activity Section 6: Multiplication with Mixed Numbers

Solve the following problems.

1. Ella Mae ran $2\frac{3}{4}$ miles in one day. Richard ran $1\frac{3}{4}$ times that amount. How many miles did Richard run?

2. McKenna lives $3\frac{7}{8}$ miles from school. The movie theater is $2\frac{1}{2}$ times as far from her house. How many miles away from McKenna's house is the movie theater?

3. Sasha collected $1\frac{3}{4}$ bins of glass jars to recycle. Emma collected $2\frac{1}{2}$ times more. How many bins of recyclables did Emma collect?

UNDERSTAND

You will use fractions often in your daily life. In the activity below, use what you know about solving real-world problems with fractions.

Activity Section

Rosa went on a $\frac{1}{2}$-hour bike ride. Her friend Tessa joined her for $\frac{1}{2}$ of that bike ride. For how long did the girls ride bikes together? How many total minutes is that?

Standardd: CCSS.Math.Content.5.NF.B.6; CCSS.Math.Practice.MP1, MP2, MP4, MP6, MP7,

DISCOVER

A multi-step problem can show you new ways to use fractions. In the activity below, use what you know about solving real-world problems with fractions.

Activity Section

The Suarez's backyard is $148\frac{1}{2}$ square feet. They have a patio that is $10\frac{1}{2}$ feet long by $5\frac{3}{4}$ feet wide. How much of their yard is not part of the patio?

CORE Dividing Fractions Concepts

Dividing Fractions and Whole Numbers

UNPACK THE STANDARD
You will divide unit fractions and whole numbers.

LEARN IT: Dividing a whole number by a fraction is the same as finding the number of parts that make up each whole. Dividing a fraction by a whole number is the same as splitting the fraction into smaller parts.

Example: Solve $3 \div \frac{1}{3}$.

You can model this with fraction strips.

Step 1: Use fraction strips to count the number of thirds that fit in 3 wholes. Note that 9 thirds fit into 3 wholes.	**Step 2:** Check your division with multiplication: $3 \div \frac{1}{3} = 9$ and $9 \times \frac{1}{3} = 3$

1			1			1		
$\frac{1}{3}$	$\frac{1}{3}$	$\frac{1}{3}$	$\frac{1}{3}$	$\frac{1}{3}$	$\frac{1}{3}$	$\frac{1}{3}$	$\frac{1}{3}$	$\frac{1}{3}$

You can model this with a number line.

Step 1: Draw a number line from 0 to 3.
Step 2: Split each whole number into thirds.

Step 3: Count how many hops (or parts) are on the number line. (9)
Step 4: Check your division with multiplication: $3 \div \frac{1}{3} = 9$ and $9 \times \frac{1}{3} = 3$

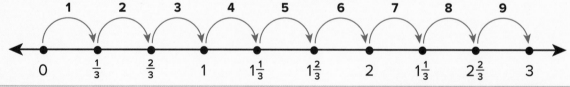

Example: Solve $\frac{1}{4} \div 2$.

You can model this with fraction strips.

Step 1: Place a $\frac{1}{4}$ strip under the whole.
Step 2: Find 2 equal fraction strips that together make $\frac{1}{4}$. Because two $\frac{1}{8}$ strips make $\frac{1}{4}$, the answer is $\frac{1}{8}$.
Step 3: Check your division with multiplication: $\frac{1}{4} \div 2 = \frac{1}{8}$ because $\frac{1}{8} \times 2 = \frac{1}{4}$

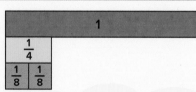

think! You match 2 strips to $\frac{1}{4}$ because you are dividing by 2. What would you do if you were dividing by 3?

Standards: CCSS.Math.Content.5.NF.B.7.B, 5.NF.B.7.C

PRACTICE: Now you try

Solve. Use multiplication to check your answer.

1. $3 \div \frac{1}{6} =$ _____ _____ × _____ = _____	**2.** $\frac{1}{4} \div 3 =$ _____ _____ × _____ = _____	**3.** $4 \div \frac{1}{4} =$ _____ _____ × _____ = _____
4. Kendall went for a 4-mile run. She stopped to stretch every $\frac{1}{2}$ of a mile. How many times did she stop? Use the expression $4 \div \frac{1}{2}$ to help.		

Morgan spent three-fourths of an hour on homework. She had assignments from 3 different classes. How much time did she spend on each assignment? Write an expression using a fraction divided by a whole number to help. Show your work and explain your thinking on a piece of paper.

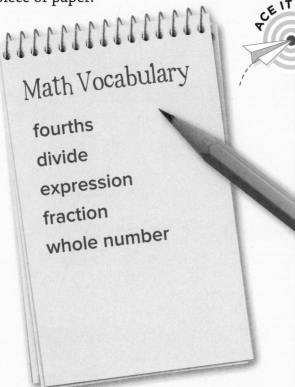

Math Vocabulary

fourths
divide
expression
fraction
whole number

ACE IT TIME!

	yes	no
Did you underline the question in the word problem?	◯	◯
Did you circle the numbers or number words?	◯	◯
Did you box the supporting details or information needed to solve the problem?	◯	◯
Did you draw a picture or a graphic organizer and write a math sentence to show your thinking?	◯	◯
Did you label your numbers and your picture?	◯	◯
Did you explain your thinking and use math vocabulary words in your explanation?	◯	◯

MATH ON THE MOVE

Have a discussion with an adult or friend. Talk about how multiplication and division are similar as well as different when you are working with fractions.

Using Models to Divide Fractions and Whole Numbers

UNPACK THE STANDARD
You will divide unit fractions and whole numbers.

LEARN IT: You can use visual models to divide fractions and whole numbers. Remember what you learned in the last lesson. Use it to solve real-world problems.

Example: You and 2 friends go to a candy shop. You decide to evenly split a $\frac{1}{4}$ pound bag of candy. How much candy will each of you get?

$\frac{1}{4} \div 3 =$ ___ pound of candy

Step 1:	Step 2:	Step 3:
Draw a rectangle to represent a bag of candy. Divide it into fourths and shade one-fourth.	Divide each fourth into 3 equal parts to represent the 3 friends!	Shade one of the thirds a new color. This is how much one friend gets.
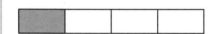		

Step 4:
The rectangle now shows 12 equal pieces. The part shaded in a new color represents how much one friend gets. It is one-twelfth ($\frac{1}{12}$).

$$\frac{1}{4} \div 3 = \frac{1}{12} \qquad \text{Check: } \frac{1}{12} \times 3 = \frac{3}{12} = \frac{1}{4}$$

Example: Omar has 9 cups of trail mix to split into $\frac{1}{3}$ cup serving sizes. How many servings can he make?

$9 \div \frac{1}{3} =$ ___ servings

Step 1:	Step 2:	Step 3:
Draw 9 rectangles.	Divide each rectangle into thirds.	Count the number of pieces.
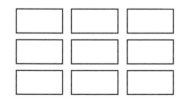	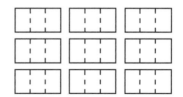	Nine wholes divided into thirds makes 27 pieces. $9 \div \frac{1}{3} = 27$ Check: $27 \times \frac{1}{3} = \frac{27}{3} = 9$

Standards: CCSS.Math.Content.5.NF.B.7.A, 5.NF.B.7.B, 5.NF.B.7.C

PRACTICE: Now you try

Solve. Use multiplication to check your answer.

1. $\frac{1}{5} \div 4 =$ Check:	2. $3 \div \frac{1}{5} =$ Check:	3. $\frac{1}{5} \div 5 =$ Check:	4. $9 \div \frac{1}{2} =$ Check:

5. There are 12 bags of pizza dough in the Walton Elementary Cooking Club. Each club member will receive $\frac{1}{5}$ of a bag of dough. For how many members can the club provide dough?

A giant tortoise can travel about $\frac{1}{3}$ foot per second. How many seconds would it take to travel 10 feet? Use multiplication to check your answer. Show your work and explain your thinking on a piece of paper.

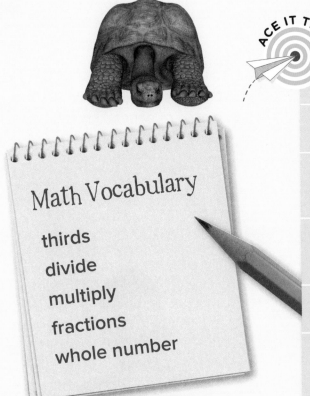

ACE IT TIME!

	yes	no
Did you underline the question in the word problem?	○	○
Did you circle the numbers or number words?	○	○
Did you box the supporting details or information needed to solve the problem?	○	○
Did you draw a picture or a graphic organizer and write a math sentence to show your thinking?	○	○
Did you label your numbers and your picture?	○	○
Did you explain your thinking and use math vocabulary words in your explanation?	○	○

Math Vocabulary

- thirds
- divide
- multiply
- fractions
- whole number

MATH ON THE MOVE

Talk about it! How can you divide fractions by solving a related multiplication sentence? Why does this work? Is the quotient greater or less than the dividend when you divide a whole number by a fraction? What about when you divide a fraction by a whole number?

Interpreting Fractions as Division

UNPACK THE STANDARD
You will understand that fractions show the numerator divided by the denominator.

LEARN IT: A fraction can be rewritten as a division problem. Remember that when you divide, you are breaking something apart into equal groups. Those groups can be whole numbers or parts, like thirds and fourths.

$$\frac{12}{6} = 12 \div 6 = 2$$
and
$$\frac{1}{2} = 1 \div 2$$

Example: There are 6 pieces of construction paper to share with 4 friends. How many pieces of paper will each friend receive?

$6 \div 4 =$ _ pieces of paper

You can draw a visual model to solve.

Step 1:	Step 2:	Step 3:
Draw 6 rectangles.	Split each rectangle into 4 pieces.	Each friend will receive $1\frac{1}{2}$ pieces of paper. This totals $\frac{6}{4}$ piece of paper per friend.
	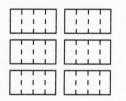	Simplify: $\frac{6}{4} = 1\frac{2}{4}$ or $1\frac{1}{2}$

You can write the division problem as a fraction and simplify.

$$6 \div 4 = \frac{6}{4} = \frac{3}{2} = 1\frac{1}{2} \text{ pieces of paper}$$

Standard: CCSS.Math.Content.5.NF.B.3

PRACTICE: Now you try

Draw the lines on the models to solve. Then, complete the next two problems.

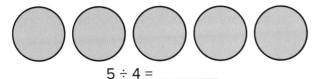

1. Four friends share 5 pizzas equally.

5 ÷ 4 = _____

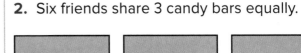

2. Six friends share 3 candy bars equally.

3 ÷ 6 = _____

3. Five students share 9 feet of rope equally.

_____ ÷ _____ = _____

4. Eight friends share 6 oranges equally.

_____ ÷ _____ = _____

think! What object are you dividing?

There are 15 members in the photography club. Mrs. Lamar has 35 index cards to use for their project. How many index cards will each club member get? Show your work and explain your thinking on a piece of paper.

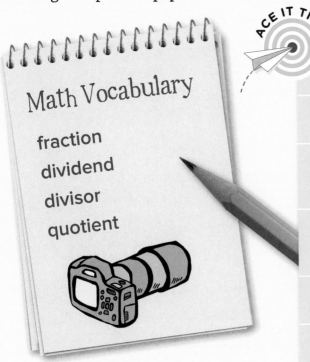

Math Vocabulary

fraction
dividend
divisor
quotient

ACE IT TIME!

	yes	no
Did you underline the question in the word problem?	○	○
Did you circle the numbers or number words?	○	○
Did you box the supporting details or information needed to solve the problem?	○	○
Did you draw a picture or a graphic organizer and write a math sentence to show your thinking?	○	○
Did you label your numbers and your picture?	○	○
Did you explain your thinking and use math vocabulary words in your explanation?	○	○

MATH ON THE MOVE

Explain how, when, and why a fraction can represent division. Think about it!

REVIEW

Congratulations! You've finished the lessons for this unit. That means you've learned how to divide a whole number by a fraction and how to divide a fraction by a whole number. You also know that you can use fractions to divide numerators and denominators.

Now it's time to prove your division skills. Solve the problems below. Use all the methods you have learned.

Activity Section 1: Dividing Fractions and Whole Numbers

Solve the following problems.

1. $\frac{3}{5} \div 6 =$	**2.** $4 \div \frac{1}{3} =$	**3.** $\frac{1}{8} \div 3 =$
4. $25 \div \frac{1}{4} =$	**5.** $\frac{1}{2} \div 10 =$	**6.** $5 \div \frac{1}{6} =$

Write a division sentence to help you solve the following problems.

7. If you divide \$3 into quarters, how many quarters will you have? *Hint:* There are 4 quarters in 1 dollar. One quarter is what fraction of a dollar?

_____ ÷ _____ = _____

8. Antonio makes 8 hoagies. He splits each hoagie into 4 pieces. How many people can he feed if each person gets 1 piece?

_____ ÷ _____ = _____

9. Amos has 5 bags of gravel. Each landscaping project uses $\frac{1}{4}$ of a bag. How many projects can he complete?

_____ ÷ _____ = _____

10. Corbin has $\frac{1}{2}$ of a piece of construction paper. If he cuts the paper in 4 equal parts to share among 4 friends, what fraction of a whole piece of paper will each friend get?

_____ ÷ _____ = _____

11. A baker cuts $\frac{1}{2}$ of a stick of butter into 3 pieces. What fraction of a whole stick of butter is in each piece?

_____ ÷ _____ = _____

Standards: CCSS.Math.Content.5.NF.B.3, 5.NF.B.7.A, 5.NF.B.7.B, 5.NF.B.7.C

Activity Section 2: Using Models to Divide Fractions and Whole Numbers

Solve the following problems.

1. $\frac{1}{7} \div 2 =$ _____ _____ × _____ = _____	**2.** $24 \div \frac{1}{2} =$ _____ _____ × _____ = _____	**3.** $\frac{1}{2} \div 5 =$ _____ _____ × _____ = _____
4. $\frac{1}{4} \div 8 =$ _____ _____ × _____ = _____	**5.** $4 \div \frac{1}{9} =$ _____ _____ × _____ = _____	**6.** $\frac{1}{3} \div 10 =$ _____ _____ × _____ = _____
7. Two friends share ½ of a watermelon equally. How much watermelon does each friend get?		
8. Shayla has 6 yards of fabric. She cuts the fabric into $\frac{1}{3}$ yard pieces. How many pieces of fabric does she have now?		
9. Gia needs 2 cups of flour for a recipe. She only has a $\frac{1}{4}$ cup measuring cup. How many times will she need to fill the $\frac{1}{4}$ cup?		

Activity Section 3: Interpreting Fractions as Division

Solve the following problems. Fill in the boxes to complete each division problem as a fraction. Simplify when needed.

1. $3 \div 6 = \dfrac{\Box}{6} = \dfrac{\Box}{\Box}$	**2.** $4 \div 5 = \dfrac{\Box}{5} = \dfrac{\Box}{\Box}$	**3.** $10 \div 12 = \dfrac{\Box}{\Box} = \dfrac{\Box}{\Box}$
4. $7 \div 4 =$	**5.** $2 \div 8 =$	**6.** $12 \div 7 =$
7. Rhianna has 3 protein bars to split among 5 people. How much of a protein bar will each person get? Draw a model to help you solve.		
8. Greg has 13 muffins. He gives them equally to four people. How many muffins does each person get? Draw a model to help you solve.		

UNDERSTAND

Understand the meaning of what you have learned and apply your knowledge.

You will have to divide with fractions often in your daily life. Use what you know about dividing fractions and whole numbers to solve the problem below.

Activity Section

Avery served brownies at her sleepover party. She had 2 pans of brownies. She cut each pan into eighths. How many brownies did she have? If everyone at the party had 2 brownies, how many people were there?

Standards: CCSS.Math.Content.5.NF.B.7.C; CCSS.Math.Practice.MP1, MP2, MP4, MP6, MP7

DISCOVER

A multi-step problem can show you new ways to use fractions. Use what you know about interpreting fractions to solve the problem below.

Activity Section

At the end-of-the-year celebration, the members of your school's Math and Science Club will split 3 pints of ice cream for every 5 students. The Student Council will split 5 pints of ice cream for every 8 students. Yuri and Nima are trying to decide which celebration would give them more ice cream. Yuri said he would rather go to the Math and Science Club celebration. Nima said she would rather celebrate with the Student Council Club. Whom do you agree with and why?

Line Plots

UNPACK THE STANDARD
You will make a line plot to answer a set of questions.

LEARN IT: Remember what you know about line plots. You can plot whole numbers on a number line. You can also plot fractions. You can use that data to answer questions.

Example: Sarah collected seashells at the beach. She measured their lengths to the nearest $\frac{1}{8}$ of an inch.

Step 1:	Step 2:
Plot the data on a line graph between 0 and 1. Split the line into eighths because the measurement of the seashells is to the nearest $\frac{1}{8}$ inch. Place an X by each number to represent each shell of that length.	Use the data on the line plot to answer questions.

Step 1:

Plot the data on a line graph between 0 and 1. Split the line into eighths because the measurement of the seashells is to the nearest $\frac{1}{8}$ inch. Place an X by each number to represent each shell of that length.

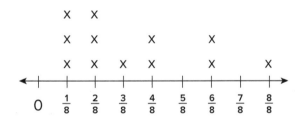

Step 2:

Use the data on the line plot to answer questions.

1. What is the difference in size from the largest shell to the smallest shell?
    $$\frac{8}{8} - \frac{1}{8} = \frac{7}{8} \text{ in.}$$

2. What is the total length of shells that measured $\frac{2}{8}$ in.?
    $$\frac{2}{8} \times 3 = \frac{6}{8} \text{ or } \frac{3}{4} \text{ in.}$$

3. If you put all the shells together from end to end, what is the total length?
    $$(3 \times \tfrac{1}{8}) + (3 \times \tfrac{2}{8}) + \tfrac{3}{8} + (2 \times \tfrac{4}{8}) +$$
    $$(2 \times \tfrac{6}{8}) + \tfrac{8}{8} = \tfrac{40}{8} = 5 \text{ in.}$$

4. What is the **average** length of the shells she found? (To find the average, divide the total length by the number of shells.)
    $$5 \div 12 = \tfrac{5}{12} \text{ in.}$$

Standard: CCSS.Math.Content.5.MD.B.2

PRACTICE: Now you try

Use the line plot below to answer the questions.

1. Which serving size of dog food did the animal shelter serve the most? How much food did the shelter serve with this serving size?

2. What is the difference in size from the largest serving size to the smallest serving size?

3. How many dogs received at least a $\frac{1}{2}$ cup serving size? *Hint:* "At least" means greater than or equal to.

4. What is the average serving size of dog food that was served at the animal shelter?

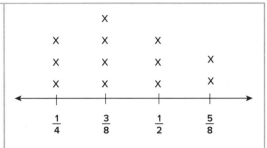

Dog Food Serving Sizes (cups)
at the Animal Shelter

Jaden measured the weights of the dwarf hamsters on sale at Frisky's Pet Shop. She recorded their weights in the following table. Put the information in a line plot and answer the questions. Remember to use your knowledge of ordering fractions! Show your work and explain your thinking on a piece of paper.

1. What is the total weight of all of the dwarf hamsters on sale? 2. What is the average weight of the dwarf hamsters at the pet store?

Weight of Dwarf Hamsters (in pounds):

$\frac{1}{4}$	$\frac{3}{8}$	$\frac{1}{2}$	$\frac{3}{4}$	$\frac{1}{2}$	$\frac{1}{4}$
$\frac{3}{4}$	$\frac{1}{2}$	$\frac{2}{8}$	$\frac{3}{8}$	1	$\frac{2}{4}$

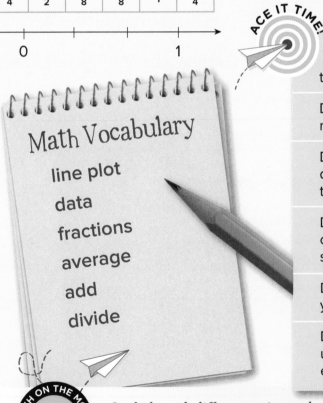

Math Vocabulary

line plot

data

fractions

average

add

divide

ACE IT TIME!

	yes	no
Did you underline the question in the word problem?	○	○
Did you circle the numbers or number words?	○	○
Did you box the supporting details or information needed to solve the problem?	○	○
Did you draw a picture or a graphic organizer and write a math sentence to show your thinking?	○	○
Did you label your numbers and your picture?	○	○
Did you explain your thinking and use math vocabulary words in your explanation?	○	○

MATH ON THE MOVE

Look through different recipes at home (or online with an adult). Notice how many teaspoons of salt each recipe calls for. Create a line plot to record the data you find. What is the average amount of salt in 10 of your favorite recipes?

Ordered Pairs and Coordinate Planes

UNPACK THE STANDARD
You will graph and name points on a coordinate plane using ordered pairs.

LEARN IT: Locating a point on a coordinate plane is a lot like reading a map. On this map, you find the points by using an x-axis and a y-axis. Look at the following coordinate grid. The *x-axis* is the horizontal line; the *y-axis* is the vertical line. Both lines meet at the point (0,0), which is called the *origin*. Each point on a coordinate grid is called an *ordered pair*.

To plot an ordered pair on a coordinate grid, follow the pattern of (x,y). The first number is on the horizontal x-axis. The second number is on the vertical y-axis.

Example: Plot (4,3).

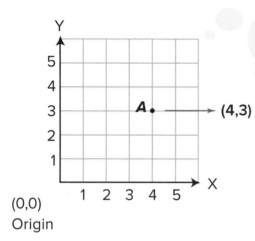

(0,0)
Origin

think! Raise your hand in the air and say "y to the sky!" This will help you remember the y-axis is vertical.

Point A shows (4,3). To plot it, start at the origin and move 4 units right on the x-axis. Then move up 3 units on the y-axis.

think! "Over and up" or "Run before you jump!"

PRACTICE: Now you try

Follow the (x,y) pattern to plot the ordered pairs on the coordinate grid.

1. (2,7)	**2.** (7,2)	**3.** (8,8)
4. (1,0)	**5.** (0,4)	**6.** (4,3)

7. Jannae's house is at the coordinate point of (5,6.) Plot this point on the grid and label it H.

8. The movie theater is at (5,9). Plot this point on the grid and label it M.

9. How many units apart are Jannae's house and the movie theater?

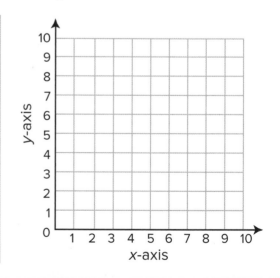

Standards: CCSS.Math.Content.5.G.A.1, 5.G.A.2

Plot the following points on the coordinate grid. After you plot each ordered pair, connect the points in the order you plotted them. What is the name of the shape you have drawn? How do you know? Show your work and explain your thinking on a piece of paper.

(6,9) (8,7) (8,5) (6,3)

(4,3) (2,5) (2,7) (4,9)

Math Vocabulary

coordinate grid

ordered pair

x-axis

y-axis

plot

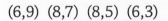

ACE IT TIME!

	yes	no
Did you underline the question in the word problem?	○	○
Did you circle the numbers or number words?	○	○
Did you box the supporting details or information needed to solve the problem?	○	○
Did you draw a picture or a graphic organizer and write a math sentence to show your thinking?	○	○
Did you label your numbers and your picture?	○	○
Did you explain your thinking and use math vocabulary words in your explanation?	○	○

MATH ON THE MOVE

Why is (3,8) not the same as (8,3)? Why do you think this is a common error for students? Can you think of ways to help you remember that the x-axis is horizontal and the y-axis is vertical?

Line Graphs

UNPACK THE STANDARD
You will create a line graph using data from a table.

LEARN IT: You can display ordered pairs in a line graph. A *line graph* is a type of graph that has points connected by a line. Below is an example of this type of graph. This line shows a change in rain over time. The coordinates representing time are on the x-axis. The points showing the amount of rain are on the y-axis. The steps show you how to make the graph.

Step 1:

Read the table. Notice the title of the table and the labels for the x- and y-axis.

Rain Collection

(x) Time (in p.m. hours)	(y) Amount of rain (in inches)
2	3
4	4
6	5
8	6

Step 2:

Rewrite the data from the table into ordered pairs.

think!
(2,3) (4,4) (6,5) (8,6)

These ordered pairs match the data in the table and follow the (x,y) pattern.

Draw a coordinate grid. Label the x- and y-axes. Give it a title.

Step 3:

Plot the points on the coordinate grid. Connect the points to make a line.

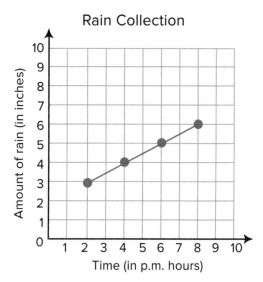

Rain Collection

Notice how the line is pointing upward. That means the amount of rain is increasing.

Step 4:

Make a statement about the data in the graph.

"This line graph shows an increase in the amount of rainfall from 2:00 p.m. to 8:00 p.m."

Standards: CCSS.Math.Content.5.G.A.1, 5.G.A.2

PRACTICE: Now you try

Follow the (x,y) pattern to plot the ordered pairs on the coordinate grid.

1. Rewrite the data from the table into ordered pairs.

Day	Height (in cm)
1	2
3	4
6	7
9	7

(_____ , _____)

(_____ , _____)

(_____ , _____)

(_____ , _____)

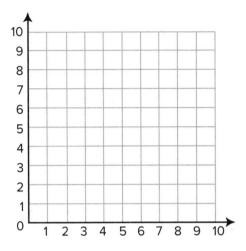

2. Label the graph with the x-axis, y-axis, and title.
3. Plot the ordered pairs.
4. Connect the points.
5. Make a statement about the growth of the plant according to the data in the graph.

Nina kept track of how much money she had saved by the end of each week. Create a graph of Nina's savings using the data listed in the table. Remember to label your graph! Show your work and explain your thinking on a piece of paper.

Week	Savings (in dollars)
1	2
2	5
3	4
4	6
5	8

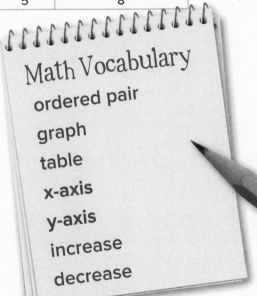

Math Vocabulary

ordered pair

graph

table

x-axis

y-axis

increase

decrease

ACE IT TIME!

	yes	no
Did you underline the question in the word problem?	○	○
Did you circle the numbers or number words?	○	○
Did you box the supporting details or information needed to solve the problem?	○	○
Did you draw a picture or a graphic organizer and write a math sentence to show your thinking?	○	○
Did you label your numbers and your picture?	○	○
Did you explain your thinking and use math vocabulary words in your explanation?	○	○

MATH ON THE MOVE

Can you think of other situations where you could collect data to display in a line graph? Why are line graphs used to show a change over time?

Identifying Numerical Patterns

UNPACK THE STANDARD

You will write and graph ordered pairs on a coordinate grid using numerical patterns.

LEARN IT: Graphs can show the relationship between numbers. Pay attention to the numbers you are graphing. Are there patterns that relate the numbers on the x-axis and y-axis?

Example: Raquel made lemonade to sell at her lemonade stand. Each serving of lemonade uses 2 tablespoons of powdered lemonade mix and 6 fluid ounces of water. The recipe can be multiplied to make more servings. The table below shows how much powdered mix and water Raquel used to make 5 pitchers of lemonade.

Step 1:

Sort the data into a table.

Pitcher	1	2	3	4	5
Mix (Tbs.)	2	4	6	8	10
Water (fl. oz)	6	12	18	24	30

Step 2:

Rewrite the data in ordered pairs.

(2,6)   (4,12)   (6,18)   (8,24)   (10,30)

Step 3:

Graph and label the ordered pairs. Label the x-axis and y-axis to match the table.

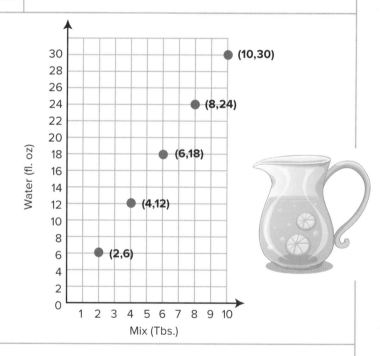

Step 4:

Write a rule to describe how the numbers in the ordered pair relate to each other.

Multiply the number of tablespoons in the mix by 3 to get the amount of water.

Standards: CCSS.Math.Content.5.G.A.2, 5.OA.B.3

PRACTICE: Now you try

Identify a pattern in the numbers. Use the pattern to finish the table.

1. Multiply the number of books by _____ to find the total spent.

Books	1	2	3	4
Total spent	8	16	24	

2. _____ the number of eggs by _____ to find the number of omelets.

Eggs	2	4	6	8
Omelets	1	2	3	

Nick is playing a video game. At the end of each level, he receives 4 gold coins and 2 extra lives. The table below shows how many gold coins and extra lives he will have after each level. **1.** Complete the table to show how many gold coins and extra lives he will have after the tenth level. **2.** Rewrite the data in ordered pairs. **3.** Write a rule to describe how the number of coins and the lives changes as Nick goes up in levels. _____

4. Graph and label the ordered pairs. Choose an appropriate scale. Show your work and explain your thinking on a piece of paper.

Level	1	2	3	4	5	10
Coins	4	8	12	16	20	
Lives	2	4	6	8	10	

ACE IT TIME!

Math Vocabulary

x-axis

y-axis

ordered pair

scale

rule

	yes	no
Did you underline the question in the word problem?	○	○
Did you circle the numbers or number words?	○	○
Did you box the supporting details or information needed to solve the problem?	○	○
Did you draw a picture or a graphic organizer and write a math sentence to show your thinking?	○	○
Did you label your numbers and your picture?	○	○
Did you explain your thinking and use math vocabulary words in your explanation?	○	○

MATH ON THE MOVE

Relationships are everywhere! Think about other number relationships you see in your life. Think about places with repetitive adding (multiplying), like when an adult puts gas in the car or buys more than one apple at the grocery store.

REVIEW

Congratulations! You've finished the lessons for this unit. That means you can make a line plot using whole numbers or fractions. You can graph and name points on a coordinate plane. You can also use data tables to create line graphs and recognize number patterns.

   Now it's time to prove your graphing skills. Solve the problems below. Use all the methods you have learned.

Activity Section 1: Line Plots

Solve the following problems.

Brittani is keeping track of how much water she drinks per day.
Use the data she collected to create a line plot.

$1\frac{1}{4}$ quarts	$2\frac{1}{4}$ quarts	2 quarts
$1\frac{1}{4}$ quarts	2 quarts	$2\frac{1}{4}$ quarts
$1\frac{1}{2}$ quarts	$1\frac{3}{4}$ quarts	$1\frac{1}{2}$ quarts
1¾ quarts	2 quarts	1½ quarts

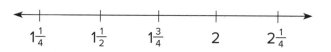

$$1\frac{1}{4} \qquad 1\frac{1}{2} \qquad 1\frac{3}{4} \qquad 2 \qquad 2\frac{1}{4}$$

Daily Water Consumption (in quarts)

1. How many days did Brittani collect data?

2. How many quarts of water did Brittani drink in all?

3. What is the difference between the greatest amount of water she drank in one day and the least amount?

4. What is the average amount of water Brittani drank each day?

5. On how many days did Brittani drink at least the average amount of water per day?

Standards: CCSS.Math.Content.5.MD.B.2, 5.G.A.1, 5.G.A.2, 5.OA.B.3

Activity Section 2: Ordered Pairs and Coordinate Planes

Solve the following problems.

Jayson made a map of his neighborhood on a coordinate grid. Each square on the grid represents one block.

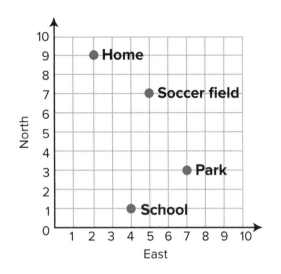

1. List the ordered pairs of the places on the map:

    School: _____

    Park: _____

    Soccer Field: _____

    Home: _____

2. What is the distance between Jayson's house and the soccer field?

3. A new pizzeria is being built at coordinate point (8,5). Plot and label this ordered pair on the map.

4. Jayson's friend Manuel lives 4 blocks north and 2 blocks west of school. Plot and label the location of his house on the map. What is the ordered pair for this spot?

5. Jayson leaves school and walks 4 blocks east then 6 blocks north. At which point on the coordinate grid does he end up?
    How far away is he from the soccer field?

Activity Section 3: Line Graphs

Answer the following questions.

1. Christina graphed the number of phone calls she received over a six-day period. Circle all of the statements below that match the graph.

   a. The number of phone calls Christina received increased by one from Day 1 to Day 2.

   b. The number of phone calls Christine received decreased the most from Day 4 to Day 5.

   c. Day 3 and Day 4 had the same number of phone calls.

   d. Day 2 and Day 6 had the same number of phone calls.

   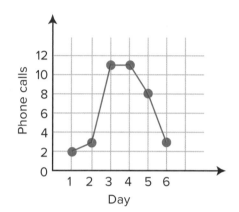

   e. The most phone calls Christina received in one day were 12.

   f. Day 2 to Day 3 had the greatest increase in phone calls.

2. Rewrite the incorrect statements above to make them correct.

3. What would be a good title for this graph?

Standards: CCSS.Math.Content.5.MD.B.2, 5.G.A.1, 5.G.A.2, 5.OA.B.3

Activity Section 4: Identifying Numerical Patterns

Solve the following problems.

1. Nico has been saving the money he earns doing chores. He chooses to spend it on downloading music, and he keeps track of how much money he spends downloading music each month. Finish the table to show how much money he will have spent on music downloads in 5 months.

Month	1	2	3	4	5
Number of songs	2	4	6	8	
Amount of money	4	8	12	16	

2. What numerical pattern, or rule, can you make from this data?

3. List the data in the table in ordered pairs.

4. Graph the ordered pairs on the coordinate grid.

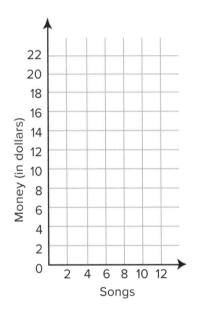

UNDERSTAND

Understand the meaning of what you have learned and apply your knowledge.

You will have to use number patterns often in your daily life. Use what you know about graphing and identifying number patterns to solve the next problem.

Activity Section

Antwon and Cole are generating patterns in math class. They have created the following tables.

Antwon's Pattern	
Term	Number
1	
2	
3	
4	
Antwon's rule: Add 4.	

Cole's Pattern	
Term	Number
1	
2	
3	
4	
Cole's rule: Add 1, and multiply by 2.	

1. Follow their rules to finish the tables.

2. List the ordered pairs in each table.

Antwon's: _____

Cole's: _____

3. Plot both sets of ordered pairs in the coordinate grid.
   Hint: You will have two separate lines: one for Antwon's data, and one for Cole's data.

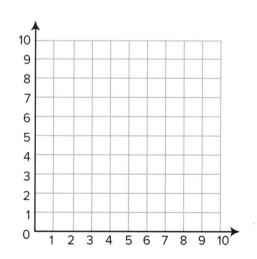

Standards: CCSS.Math.Content.5.MD.G.A.2, 5.OA.B.3; CCSS.Math.Practice.MP1, MP2, MP4, MP6, MP7, MP8

DISCOVER

Discover how you can apply the information you have learned.

Graphic data in a number line can help you see change over time. Use what you know about creating line graphs to solve the following.

Activity Section

Chantell keeps track of how many songs she downloads to her smartphone each month. She creates a table to show her data. List the ordered pairs from the data in the table and create a line graph. Remember to label and title your graph!

Chantell's Song Downloads	
Month	# of Songs
1	2
2	4
3	5
4	4
5	4

Ordered Pairs:

Write three statements to match your graph.

1. _____

_____

2. _____

_____

3. _____

_____

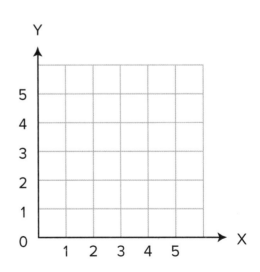

CORE Converting Units of Measurement Concepts

Customary Units of Length and Weight

UNPACK THE STANDARD
You will compare and convert measurements of length and weight.

LEARN IT: These tables show Customary Units of Length and Weight. Use these tables to compare and contrast measurements.

Customary Units of Length
1 foot (ft) = 12 inches (in.)
1 yard (yd) = 3 feet
1 mile (mi) = 5,280 feet
1 mile = 1,760 yards

Remember this tip when converting numbers:

• When converting from a larger unit to a smaller unit, you multiply.

• When converting from a smaller unit to a larger unit, you divide.

Example: 48 inches = _ feet

Step 1:	Step 2:	Step 3:
Decide which operation to use.	Decide which numbers to use.	Solve to convert!
think! Inches are smaller than feet. You are going from a smaller unit to a larger unit.	**think!** There are 12 inches in 1 foot, so we will divide 48 inches by 12.	48 ÷ 12 = 4 48 inches = 4 feet

You can do the same when converting units of weight.

Use this table to help you follow the same steps as above.

Example: 4 lbs = _ oz

Customary Units of Weight
1 pound (lb) = 16 ounces (oz)
1 ton (T) = 2,000 pounds

think! Pounds are larger than ounces. You are going from a larger unit to a smaller unit.

There are 16 oz in 1 lb
4 lbs x 16 = 64
4 lbs = 64 oz

Remember: When you compare, be sure to convert first so you are comparing the same unit!

Standard: CCSS.Math.Content.5.MD.A.1

PRACTICE: Now you try

Convert using the tables on page 142.

1. 4 ft. = _____ in.	**2.** 72 in. = _____ yd	**3.** 2 mi = _____ ft.	**4.** 18 ft. = _____ yd
5. 5,280 ft. = _____ mi	**6.** 60 in. = _____ ft.	**7.** 5 lb 3 oz = _____ oz	**8.** 3 T = _____ lb

Compare the measurements and fill in the circle with >, <, or =.

9. 3 yd ◯ 3 ft.	**10.** 1 ft. 8 in. ◯ 22 in.	**11.** 3 mi ◯ 5,280 yd
12. 4 ft. 5 in. ◯ 45 in.	**13.** 15 ft. ◯ 6 yd	**14.** 1,800 oz ◯ 100 lb

Mrs. Baker's classroom is 32 feet long. Mrs. Peter's classroom is 9 yards 6 inches long. Whose classroom is longer? How do you know? Show your work and explain your thinking on a piece of paper.

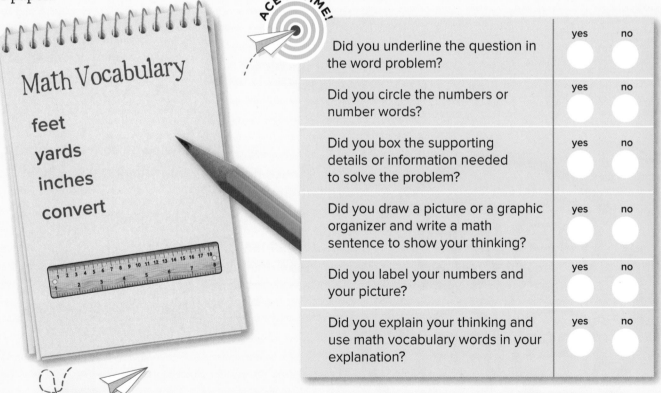

Math Vocabulary

feet
yards
inches
convert

ACE IT TIME!

	yes	no
Did you underline the question in the word problem?	◯	◯
Did you circle the numbers or number words?	◯	◯
Did you box the supporting details or information needed to solve the problem?	◯	◯
Did you draw a picture or a graphic organizer and write a math sentence to show your thinking?	◯	◯
Did you label your numbers and your picture?	◯	◯
Did you explain your thinking and use math vocabulary words in your explanation?	◯	◯

MATH ON THE MOVE

Look for places in daily life that use Customary Units of Length or Weight. Food packaging is a great place to look. For example, a box of pasta usually weighs 1 pound. How many ounces is that? How many ounces would 2 boxes weigh?

Customary Units of Capacity

UNPACK THE STANDARD
You will compare and convert measurements of capacity.

LEARN IT: *Capacity* is the amount of liquid a container can hold. Use this next table to help you compare and convert capacity measurements. The same rules apply when converting measurements:

- When converting from a larger unit to a smaller unit, you multiply.

- When converting from a smaller unit to a larger unit, you divide.

Customary Units of Capacity
1 cup (c) = 8 fluid ounces (fl. oz)
1 pint (pt) = 2 cups
1 quart (qt) = 2 pints
1 gallon (gal) = 4 quarts

Example: 3 pints = _ cups

Step 1:	Step 2:	Step 3:
Decide which operation to use.	Decide which numbers to use.	Solve to convert!
think! Converting from pints to cups is going from a larger to a smaller unit.	**think!** There are 2 cups in 1 pint.	3 pints × 2 = 6 3 pints = 6 cups

"The Giant G" can help you convert capacity:

Notice how inside the "Giant G" (or gallon) there are 4 quarts.

Inside each quart are 2 pints.

Inside each pint are 2 cups.

How many fluid ounces would you write in each "C"?

Standard: CCSS.Math.Content.5.MD.A.1

PRACTICE: Now you try

Convert using the tables on page 144.

1. 1 qt = _____ pt	**2.** 3 gal = _____ qt	**3.** 6 c = _____ pt	**4.** 2 gal = _____ cups
5. 16 pt = _____ gal	**6.** 16 fl. oz = _____ c	**7.** 4 qt = _____ pt	**8.** 9 gal = _____ pt

Compare the amounts. Use >, <, or =.

9. 16 fl. oz ◯ 1 pt	**10.** 42 qt ◯ 12 gal	**11.** 12 pt ◯ 8 qt

Martez sold 8 quarts of lemonade at his lemonade stand. His sister sold 3 gallons. Who sold more lemonade? How much more? How do you know? Show your work and explain your thinking on a piece of paper.

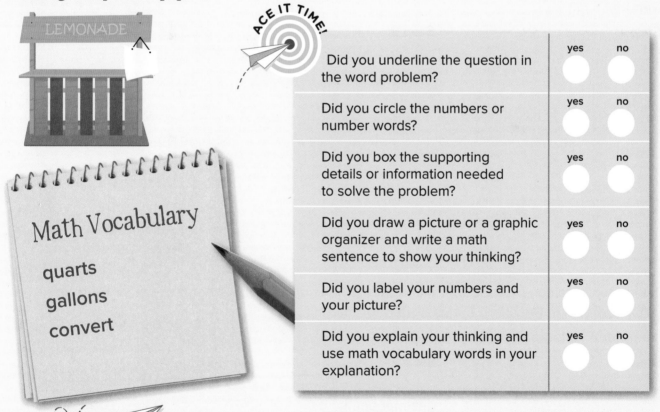

ACE IT TIME!

	yes	no
Did you underline the question in the word problem?	◯	◯
Did you circle the numbers or number words?	◯	◯
Did you box the supporting details or information needed to solve the problem?	◯	◯
Did you draw a picture or a graphic organizer and write a math sentence to show your thinking?	◯	◯
Did you label your numbers and your picture?	◯	◯
Did you explain your thinking and use math vocabulary words in your explanation?	◯	◯

Math Vocabulary

quarts

gallons

convert

MATH ON THE MOVE

Doctors and other health officials recommend that children ages 9-12 should drink seven 8 oz glasses of water each day. Bottled water is sold in 16.9 fl. oz servings. About how many bottles of water should you drink each day to reach the recommended serving?

Metric Units of Length and Weight

UNPACK THE STANDARD
You will convert measurements with metric units of length and weight.

LEARN IT: The metric system of measurement is based on powers of 10. To convert, use what you know about multiplying and dividing by powers of 10. You can also use the prefixes in the following chart to help you.

kilo-	hecto-	deca-	UNIT	deci-	centi-	milli-
(k)	(h)	(da)	**meter** (length)	(d)	(c)	(m)
1,000	100	10	**gram** (weight)	0.1	0.01	0.001

To convert from **larger** to **smaller**, move the decimal point to the right **(multiply)**. ⟶

⟵ To convert from **smaller** to **larger**, move the decimal point to the left **(divide)**.

Example: 5 cm = _

Step 1:	Step 2:	Step 3:
Decide which operation to use. **think!** Converting from centimeter to meter is going from smaller to larger.	Decide where to move the decimal point. **think!** Meters are 2 places away from centimeters. Move the decimal point 2 places to the left to divide.	Convert. 1 m = 100 cm 5 ÷ 100 = 0.05 5cm= 0.05 m

Step 3 table:

METER	deci-	centi-
		5.
0.	.0	.5

The decimal point moves 2 places to the left.

The same steps can be used to convert metric units of weight. Remember to use the same prefixes shown in the chart, but use **gram** for the unit.

Example: 25 kilograms = _ grams

Step 1:	Step 2:	Step 3:
Decide which operation to use. **think!** Converting from kilograms to grams is going from larger to smaller.	Decide where to move the decimal point. **think!** Grams are 3 places away from kilograms, so we will move the decimal point 3 places to the right to multiply.	Convert. 1 kg = 1,000 g 1,000 x 25 = 25,000 25 kg = 25,000 g

Standard: CCSS.Math.Content.5.MD.A.1

PRACTICE: Now you try

Convert using the tables on page 146.

1. 1,000 mg = _____ g	**2.** 4 cm = _____ mm	**3.** 350 m = _____ km	**4.** 8 km = _____ m
5. 26 km = _____ m	**6.** 450 cm = _____ m	**7.** 12 mm = _____ cm	**8.** 3.5 kg = _____ g

Micah rescued a puppy from the Sunshine Animal Shelter. His veterinarian says the puppy weighs 5,000 grams. Micah wants to know how many kilograms that is. Help Micah convert to kilograms. Show your work and explain your thinking on a piece of paper.

ACE IT TIME!

Math Vocabulary

kilograms

grams

convert

metric system

units

	yes	no
Did you underline the question in the word problem?	○	○
Did you circle the numbers or number words?	○	○
Did you box the supporting details or information needed to solve the problem?	○	○
Did you draw a picture or a graphic organizer and write a math sentence to show your thinking?	○	○
Did you label your numbers and your picture?	○	○
Did you explain your thinking and use math vocabulary words in your explanation?	○	○

MATH ON THE MOVE

Why do you think you have learned both the Customary Units of Measurement and the Metric System? Which system is more popular in the United States? Ask an adult to help you visit the following website to read about how and why scientists all over the world use the metric system: *http://kids.niehs.nih.gov/explore/scienceworks/science_metric_system.htm*

Metric Units of Capacity

UNPACK THE STANDARD
You will convert measurements with metric units of capacity.

LEARN IT: Think about what you have learned about the metric system. Converting metric units of capacity is the same as converting metric units of length and weight. The base unit is *liter (L)*, but the prefixes are the same as other metric units.

kilo-	hecto-	deca-	UNIT	deci-	centi-	milli-
(k)	(h)	(da)	**liter** (capacity)	(d)	(c)	(m)
1,000	100	10	(L)	0.1	0.01	0.001

To convert from **larger** to **smaller**, move the decimal point to the right **(multiply).** ⟶

⟵ To convert from **smaller** to **larger**, move the decimal point to the left **(divide).**

Example: 8 mL= _ L

Step 1:	Step 2:	Step 3:
Decide which operation to use. **think!** Converting from milliliter to liter is going from smaller to larger.	Decide where to move the decimal point. **think!** Milliliters are 3 places away from liters. Move the decimal point 3 places to the left to divide.	Convert. 1 L = 1,000 mL 8 ÷ 1,000 8 mL = 0.008 L

Step 3 table:

LITER	deci-	centi-	milli-
			8.
0.	.0	.0	8

The decimal point moves 3 places to the left.

Standard: CCSS.Math.Content.5.MD.A.1

PRACTICE: Now you try

Convert the following metric units of capacity.

1. 16 L = _____ mL	**2.** 4.25 kL = _____ daL	**3.** 50 mL = _____ L	**4.** 8,000 cL = _____ hL

Compare the following measurements. Fill in the blank with >, <, or =.

5. 1.4 L ◯ 140 mL	**6.** 525 mL ◯ 52.5 cL	**7.** 48 hL ◯ 0.048 kL

Ashanti measured the liquid left in the beakers of her science classroom. She collected a total of 750 mL. Is that more or less than 7.5 L? How do you know? Show your work and explain your thinking on a piece of paper.

 ACE IT TIME!

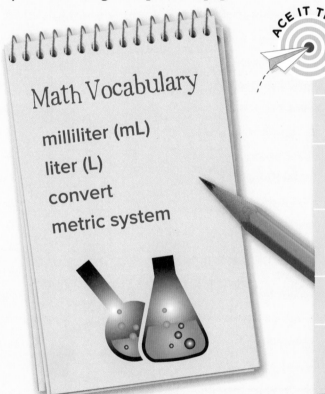

Math Vocabulary

milliliter (mL)
liter (L)
convert
metric system

	yes	no
Did you underline the question in the word problem?	◯	◯
Did you circle the numbers or number words?	◯	◯
Did you box the supporting details or information needed to solve the problem?	◯	◯
Did you draw a picture or a graphic organizer and write a math sentence to show your thinking?	◯	◯
Did you label your numbers and your picture?	◯	◯
Did you explain your thinking and use math vocabulary words in your explanation?	◯	◯

 **MATH ON THE MOVE**

You can use the mnemonic "King Henry Did Usually Drink Chocolate Milk" to help you memorize and recall the order of the metric prefixes. Can you see why? Try making up your own mnemonic to help you remember the order!

Elapsed Time

UNPACK THE STANDARD
You will convert units of time to answer questions about elapsed time.

LEARN IT: *Elapsed time* is the amount of time that has passed after giving a fixed starting point. You can solve elapsed-time problems by converting measurements.

> **think!** Remember:
> larger to smaller = multiply
> smaller to larger = divide

Example: Julia's laptop has 3 hours and 15 minutes of battery life remaining. How many minutes does she have left before she needs to charge it?

Step 1:
Decide which unit you need to convert to. This question is asking you to find how many minutes, so you are converting from hours to minutes.

> **think!** Hours are larger than minutes.

Step 2:
Convert. 3 hours × 60 = 180 minutes 3 hours and 15 minutes = 180 + 15 = 195 minutes

> **think!**
> 60 minutes = 1 hour

You can also use a number line to answer questions about elapsed time.

Example: Frank's soccer practice started at 10:30 a.m. on Saturday. It lasted 2 ½ hours. What time did practice finish?

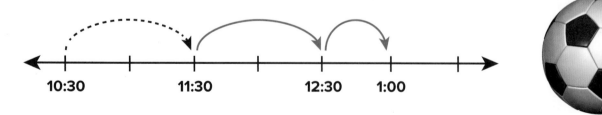

Step 1:	Step 2:	Step 3:
Start at 10:30 on the number line.	Hop 2 hours.	Hop ½ hour. Frank's soccer practice finished at 1:00 p.m.

Standard: CCSS.Math.Content.5.MD.A.1

PRACTICE: Now you try

Use the table to convert.

1. 310 min = _____ hr _____ min.	**2.** 4 hr 15 min = _____ min
3. 52 hr = _____ d _____ hr	**4.** 60 mo = _____ yr
5. 30 d = _____ wk _____ d	**6.** 6 wk = _____ d

Units of Time
60 seconds (sec) = 1 minute (min)
60 min = 1 hour (hr)
24 hr = 1 day (d)
7 d = 1 week (wk)
52 wk = 1 year (yr)
12 months (mo) = 1 yr
365 d = 1 yr

Nigel played all of the songs on one of his playlists. He started listening at 11:30 a.m. The playlist lasted 85 minutes. What time did the playlist end? Show your work and explain your thinking on a piece of paper.

ACE IT TIME!

	yes	no
Did you underline the question in the word problem?	◯	◯
Did you circle the numbers or number words?	◯	◯
Did you box the supporting details or information needed to solve the problem?	◯	◯
Did you draw a picture or a graphic organizer and write a math sentence to show your thinking?	◯	◯
Did you label your numbers and your picture?	◯	◯
Did you explain your thinking and use math vocabulary words in your explanation?	◯	◯

Math Vocabulary

elapsed time

minutes

hours

convert

MATH ON THE MOVE

Think of all the times you solve elapsed time problems each day. There are probably too many to count! Make an elapsed-time problem based on what time it is right now. For example, "It is 3:30 p.m. How many hours do you have until bedtime?"

REVIEW

Congratulations! You've finished the lessons for this unit. That means you can convert customary units of length and weight. You can also convert measurements of capacity. You can work within the metric system, too, and calculate elapsed time.

Now it's time to prove your measuring and converting skills. Solve the following problems. Use all the methods you have learned.

Activity Section 1: Customary Units of Length and Weight

Solve the following problems.

1. Jade and Katy competed in the long jump at the track meet. Jade's jump measured 108 inches, and Katy's jump measured 3.5 yards. Who jumped farther?

2. Mr. Cohen is fixing his children's swing set. He needs 6 feet of wood to complete the sides, and 65 inches of wood to complete the top. How many feet of wood does he need to complete the entire project?

3. The Brooklyn Bridge has a maximum weight limit of 80,000 pounds. How many tons is that?

4. Maria went to her older brother's football game. His team ran a play for 34 yards. How many feet is that?

5. Kara's cat weighs 13 pounds, 4 ounces. Michelle's cat weighs 192 ounces. Which cat weighs more?

Standard: CCSS.Math.Content.5.MD.A.1

Activity Section 2: Customary Units of Capacity

Solve the following problems.

1. Michaela buys 2 quarts of orange juice to serve at the volunteer breakfast at her school. How many 1-cup servings will that provide?

2. How many pints of ice cream are equal to 1 gallon? Two gallons? Three gallons?

3. Zane bought 2 gallons of paint to mix with the 3 quarts he already had. How many quarts of paint does he have in all?

4. Steve tries to drink eight 8-fluid ounces of water each day. How many cups of water is that?

5. Colette's dog drank $1\frac{1}{2}$ gallons of water in one week. How many quarts is that?

Activity Section 3: Metric Units of Length and Weight

Solve the following problems.

1. Noah lives 8.5 kilometers from Daytona Beach. How many meters is that?

2. Randi and Nate had a paper airplane flying contest. Randi's paper airplane flew 3.5 meters; Nate's flew 40 decimeters. Whose paper airplane flew the farther distance?

3. Charley collects fall leaves. One leaf measured 32 cm long. How many mm is that?

4. Corbett drew one line segment that is 42 mm long, and another one that is 24 cm long. How many cm long are both line segments together?

5. Jacob's laptop weighs 1.34 kg. How many grams does it weigh?

Standard: CCSS.Math.Content.5.MD.A.1

Activity Section 4: Metric Units of Capacity

Solve the following problems.

1. Eduardo bought a 2-liter bottle of ginger ale. How many milliliters is that?

2. The fifth-grade science lab at Walker Elementary contained 3 beakers of 25 mL. Is that more or less than 250 cL?

3. Hand sanitizer is sold in 236 mL bottles. How many centiliters is that?

4. How many liters is 400 hectoliters?

5. Which is greater—45.8 daL or 458 dL?

Activity Section 5: Elapsed Time

Solve the following problems.

1. It takes Morgan 12 minutes to walk to her bus stop. How many seconds does it take to walk to her bus stop?

2. If Emory starts her bike ride at 8:45 a.m. and she rides for 1 hour and 10 minutes, what time is she done with her bike ride?

3. Alisa spends 1 hour and 35 minutes watching 2 podcasts. How many minutes does she spend watching the podcasts?

4. If a movie starts at 11:20 a.m. and is 95 minutes long, what time does the movie end?

5. Ben is going on a vacation by car with his family. They arrive at their destination at 4:15 p.m. after driving for 6 hours and 45 minutes. What time did they leave the house?

Standard: CCSS.Math.Content.5.MD.A.1

UNDERSTAND

You will have to calculate elapsed time often in your daily life. Use what you know about converting units of time to solve the problem below.

Activity Section

The students of the Bayside Elementary science club are presenting their experiments at their school's Science Night. Each presentation lasts 15 minutes. They do 4 presentations and take a 5-minute break after each presentation to clean up. If they start at 5:30 p.m., what time will they finish? How many hours did they spend on their presentations?

DISCOVER

Discover how you can apply the information you have learned.

Converting measurements is a useful tool for daily life. Use what you know about customary units of length and weight to solve the problem below.

Activity Section

Landon runs five 20-yard sprints at soccer practice. If he continues his practice this way, how many practices will it take for Landon to sprint a total of 2 miles? Landon thinks it will take him less than 20 practices. Do you agree with him? Why or why not?

Standards: CCSS.Math.Content.5.MD.A.1, CCSS.Math.Practice.MP1, MP2, MP3, MP4, MP6,MP7

Classifying Two-Dimensional Figures

UNPACK THE STANDARD
You will classify two-dimensional figures.

LEARN IT: There are many types of two-dimensional figures. Two-dimensional figures that have three or more sides are called polygons. Polygons with four sides are called *quadrilaterals.*

Name:	Properties:	Example:
parallelogram	Opposite sides are congruent and parallel	
rectangle	Parallelogram with 4 perpendicular sides	
square	Parallelogram with 4 congruent sides that are perpendicular	
rhombus	Parallelogram with 4 congruent sides	
trapezoid	Quadrilateral with only 1 pair of parallel sides	

Remember these vocabulary words from fourth grade?

congruent: same size, same shape

parallel: two lines that never meet

perpendicular: two lines that intersect to form a 90 degree angle

Regular polygons have all sides and angles congruent.

think! Is a regular rectangle possible?

PRACTICE: Now you try

Use the information on page 159 to help you answer.

1. A trapezoid has 2 sides parallel, so it is a parallelogram. True or False? Explain.

2. A rhombus is a rectangle. True or False? Explain.

3. A parallelogram has 4 equal sides with both sets of opposite sides parallel. True or False? Explain.

4. Regular polygons have all congruent sides and angles. True or False? Explain.

5. A square is a rectangle. True or False? Explain.

6. A rectangle is a square. True or False? Explain.

7. Perpendicular lines never meet. True or False? Explain.

8. A parallelogram has 4 sets of parallel sides. True or False? Explain.

Standards: CCSS.Math.Content.5.G.B.3, 5.G.B.4

Isaac says all rhombi are squares, and Izzy says all squares are rhombi. Who do you agree with and why? Remember, "rhombi" is plural for rhombus! Show your work and explain your thinking on a piece of paper.

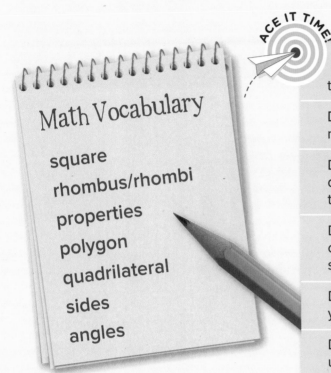

Math Vocabulary

square

rhombus/rhombi

properties

polygon

quadrilateral

sides

angles

ACE IT TIME!

	yes	no
Did you underline the question in the word problem?	○	○
Did you circle the numbers or number words?	○	○
Did you box the supporting details or information needed to solve the problem?	○	○
Did you draw a picture or a graphic organizer and write a math sentence to show your thinking?	○	○
Did you label your numbers and your picture?	○	○
Did you explain your thinking and use math vocabulary words in your explanation?	○	○

MATH ON THE MOVE

Guess my polygon! Share riddles with a friend, such as, "I am a quadrilateral with only one pair of parallel sides." Have your friend give the answer (trapezoid). Take turns creating and sharing with each other.

Exploring Volume

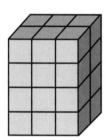

UNPACK THE STANDARD
You will find the volume of a solid figure.

LEARN IT: *Volume* is the amount of space a figure takes up. It is measured in *cubic units*, or *units³*.

You can count the number of unit cubes that fill a solid figure to find the volume.

think! This rectangular prism has a front layer with 12 cubes. Its total volume is 2 layers of 12 cubes, or 24 cubic units.

Imagine filling up this cereal box with layers of unit cubes. The total number of cubes you used would be the volume of the box!

PRACTICE: Now you try

Count the number of unit cubes to find the volume.

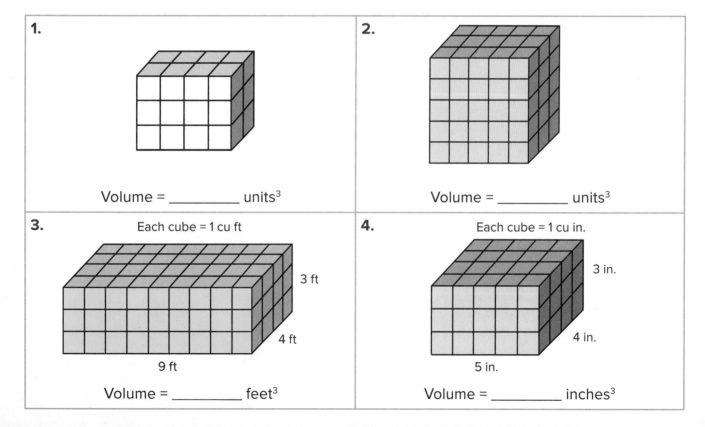

1.

Volume = _____ units³

2.

Volume = _____ units³

3. Each cube = 1 cu ft

3 ft
4 ft
9 ft

Volume = _____ feet³

4. Each cube = 1 cu in.

3 in.
4 in.
5 in.

Volume = _____ inches³

Standards: CCSS.Math.Content.5.MD.C.3.A, 5.MD.C.3.B, MD.C.4

5. Danny builds a tower out of unit cubes that is 3 cubes long, 3 cubes wide, and 3 cubes high. What is the volume of his tower?

6. Henry packed a small box with unit cubes. He could fit 12 cubes in each layer. He filled it with 4 layers. What is the volume of the box?

Arianna and Sal both have 12 unit cubes. Arianna builds a tower that is 2 cubes wide and 6 cubes high. Sal builds a tower that is 6 cubes long and 2 cubes wide. Arianna says her rectangular prism has a greater volume. Sal says both towers have the same volume. Who is correct? How do you know? Show your work and explain your thinking on a piece of paper.

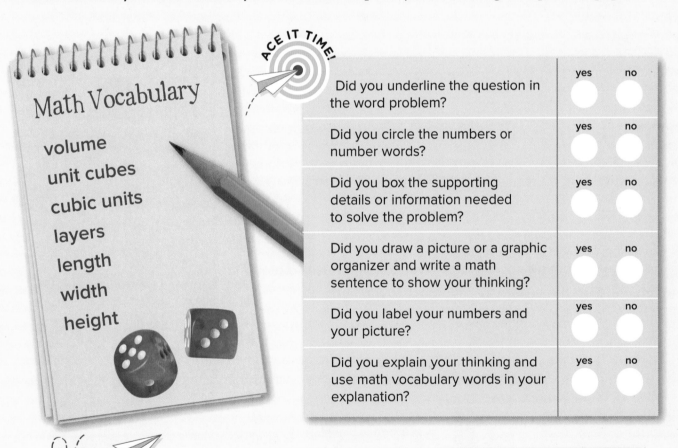

Math Vocabulary

- volume
- unit cubes
- cubic units
- layers
- length
- width
- height

ACE IT TIME!

	yes	no
Did you underline the question in the word problem?	○	○
Did you circle the numbers or number words?	○	○
Did you box the supporting details or information needed to solve the problem?	○	○
Did you draw a picture or a graphic organizer and write a math sentence to show your thinking?	○	○
Did you label your numbers and your picture?	○	○
Did you explain your thinking and use math vocabulary words in your explanation?	○	○

MATH ON THE MOVE

Roll the dice! Roll the dice three times. Each number will be one of the dimensions of a rectangular prism you will draw (or imagine!). For example, you roll a 3, 5, and 2. Your prism could be 3 cubes long by 5 cubes wide by 2 cubes high. Find the volume.

Apply Formulas to Find Volume

UNPACK THE STANDARD

You will use a formula to find the volume of rectangular prisms and solid figures composed of two rectangular prisms.

LEARN IT: The formula for volume is length times width times height. $V = l \times w \times h$

Example: Find the volume of a cube that is 7 inches by 5 inches by 3 inches.

Step 1:	Step 2:	Step 3:
Identify the length, width, and height of the rectangular prism.	Insert the numbers into the formula. volume = length × width × height OR $V = 7 \times 5 \times 3$	Solve. $V = 7$ in. $\times 5$ in. $\times 3$ in. $V = 105$ inches^3 Remember to cube your units in your answer!

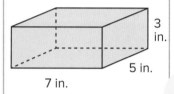

length = 7 in.

width = 5 in.

height = 3 in.

think! Volume is how much space an object takes up. We can find the volume of rectangular prisms by using the measurement of each side when we don't know how many cubes can fit inside.

You can also find the volume of two rectangular prisms combined.

Example: Find the volume of the figure to the right..

Step 1:	Step 2:	Step 3:	Step 4
Imagine breaking the figure apart into two rectangular prisms. Notice the width of the green and blue prisms are the same!	Find the length, width, and height of both rectangular prisms.	Apply the formula to find the volume of each prism. Green prism: $V = 4$ in. $\times 2$ in. $\times 4$ in. $V = 32$ in.^{3} Blue prism: $V = 10$ in. $\times 4$ in. $\times 2$ in. $V = 80$ inches^3	Add to find the total volume. 32 in.^{3} + 80 in.^{3} = 112 in.^{3}

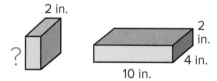

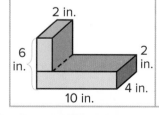

think! The total height of both prisms is 6 inches. The height of the blue prism is 2 inches. Subtract 6 − 2 = 4 inches to find the height of the green prism.

Standard: CCSS.Math.Content.5.MD.C.5.A, 5.MD.C.5.B, 5.MD.C.5.C

PRACTICE: Now you try

Use the formula to find the volume.

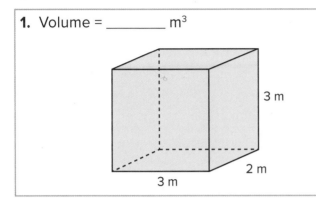

1. Volume = _____ m³

3 m

2 m

3 m

2. Volume = _____ ft³

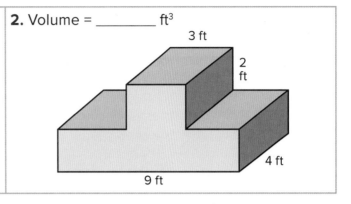

3 ft

2 ft

4 ft

9 ft

For her Earth Day recycling project, Jalen made a structure out of the two rice boxes shown below. Draw a structure Jalen could have made with the two boxes, and find the volume of her new structure. Show your work and explain your thinking on a piece of paper.

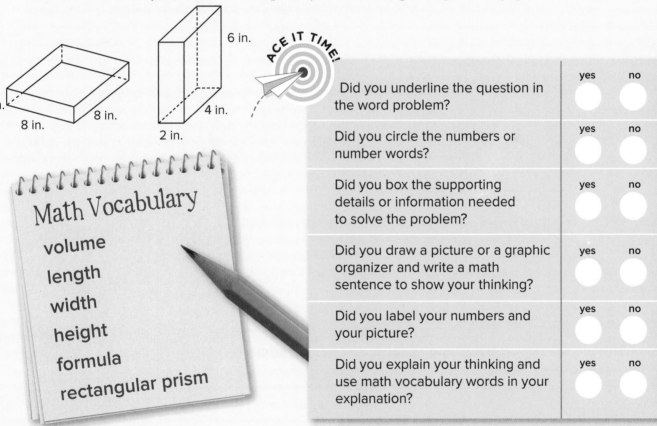

2 in.

8 in.

8 in.

6 in.

4 in.

2 in.

ACE IT TIME!

Math Vocabulary

volume

length

width

height

formula

rectangular prism

	yes	no
Did you underline the question in the word problem?	○	○
Did you circle the numbers or number words?	○	○
Did you box the supporting details or information needed to solve the problem?	○	○
Did you draw a picture or a graphic organizer and write a math sentence to show your thinking?	○	○
Did you label your numbers and your picture?	○	○
Did you explain your thinking and use math vocabulary words in your explanation?	○	○

MATH ON THE MOVE

Use number cards 1–9. Flip over three cards. Use those numbers as the dimensions of a rectangular prism, and find the volume using the formula V = l × w × h. The choice of unit is up to you, as long as the answer is cubic!

REVIEW

Congratulations! You've finished the lessons for this unit. That means you can classify parallelograms. You can find the volume of a rectangular prism using unit cubes and formulas. You can also find the volume of two rectangular prisms combined.

Now it's time to prove your geometry skills. Solve the following problems. Use all the methods you have learned.

Activity Section 1: Classifying Two-Dimensional Figures

Name each polygon in as many ways as you can.

1.

2.

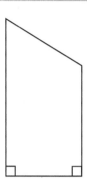

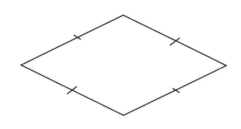

3.

4.

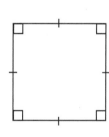

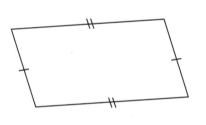

Complete the sentences by writing *always*, *sometimes,* or *never*.

5. A square is _____ a rectangle.

A rectangle is _____ a square.

A square is _____ a rhombus.

A rhombus is _____ a square.

A trapezoid is _____ a parallelogram.

A parallelogram is _____ a rectangle.

 Standards: CCSS.Math.Content.5.G.B.3, 5.G.B.4, 5.MD.C.3 .A, 5.MD.C.3.B, 5.MD.C.4 , 5.MD.C.5.A, 5.MD.C.5.B, 5.MD.C.5.C

Activity Section 2: Exploring Volume

Find the volume of each structure by counting the cubes. Compare using >, <, or =.

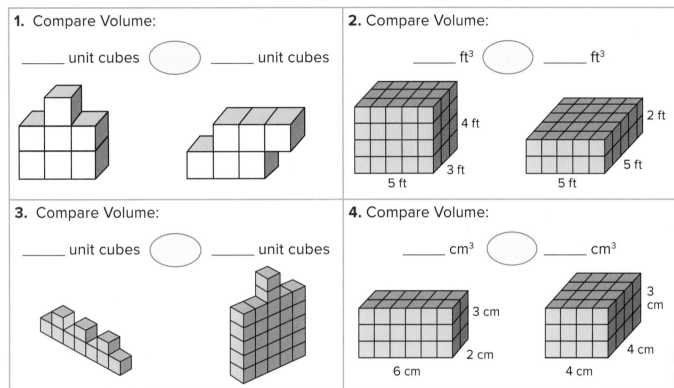

1. Compare Volume:

_____ unit cubes ◯ _____ unit cubes

2. Compare Volume:

_____ ft³ ◯ _____ ft³

4 ft

3 ft

5 ft

2 ft

5 ft

5 ft

3. Compare Volume:

_____ unit cubes ◯ _____ unit cubes

4. Compare Volume:

_____ cm³ ◯ _____ cm³

3 cm

2 cm

6 cm

3 cm

4 cm

4 cm

Activity Section 3: Apply Formulas to Find Volume

Use the formula V = l × w × h to find the volume for the next problems.

1. Jaime finds an old trunk in his grandfather's attic. It is 3 feet long by 2 feet wide and 1 foot high. What is the volume of the trunk?

2. A large aquarium at the dentist's office is 6 feet long, 2 feet wide, and 4 feet tall. To figure out how much water it holds, first you need to find the volume of the aquarium. What is the volume?

3. Corbin is moving and is packing up his video gaming system. It measures 12 inches long, 8 inches wide, and 2 inches high. The box he wants to use has a volume of 200 cubic inches. Is it big enough to hold the gaming system? How do you know?

4. Gabriela got a new puppy. The puppy sleeps in a crate at night. The volume of the crate is 12 cubic feet. The crate is 2 feet wide by 3 feet long. How tall is the crate? How do you know?

Use the formula V = l × w × h to find the volume for the next problems.

5.

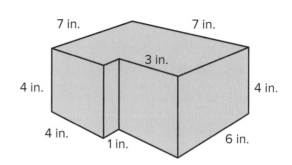

5 yd
2 yd
5 yd
5 yd
7 yd
5 yd
1 yd

Prism #1:

Length =

Width =

Height =

Volume =

Prism #2:

Length =

Width =

Height =

Volume =

Total Volume:

6.

7 in.   7 in.
3 in.
4 in.   4 in.
4 in.
1 in.   6 in.

Prism #1:

Length =

Width =

Height =

Volume =

Prism #2:

Length =

Width =

Height =

Volume =

Total Volume:

Standards: CCSS.Math.Content.5.G.B.3, 5.G.B.4, 5.MD.C.3 .A, 5.MD.C.3.B, 5.MD.C.4 , 5.MD.C.5.A, 5.MD.C.5.B, 5.MD.C.5.C

UNDERSTAND

Understand the meaning of what you have learned and apply your knowledge.

You will have to calculate volume in your daily life. Use what you know about calculating the volume of rectangular prisms to solve the problem below.

Activity Section

A packing store sells boxes and crates in different sizes. They keep the measurements of each box or crate in a table like the one shown here. Find the missing measurements to complete the table.

Length	Width	Height	Volume
3 in.	4 in.	2 in.	
	5 ft.	3 ft.	15 cubic ft.
4 m		2 m	24 m³
	6 yd	2 yd	48 cubic yd
6 cm		4 cm	72 cm³
			36 cubic ft.
			45 yd³

Explain how you got your answers:

4+4=
?

DISCOVER

Discover how you can apply the information you have learned.

Finding volume is a useful tool for daily life. Use what you know about volume formulas to solve the problem below.

Activity Section

Tonya is making furniture for her doll house. She uses a small cardboard box that measures 10 inches long, 4 inches wide, and 6 inches high. To make a miniature bed for her house, she cut out a section of the box, as shown below.

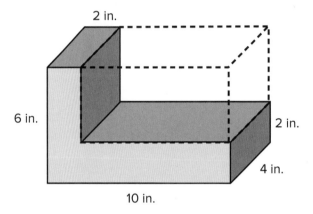

1. What is the volume of this new figure, after she cuts out the section?

2. What is the volume of the empty space (or the section she cut out)?

3. What was the total volume of the whole box before she cut the section out?

Standards: CCSS.Math.Content.5.MD.C.5.A, 5.MD.C.5.B, 5.MD.C.5.C; CCSS.Math.Practice.MP1, MP2, MP4, MP6, MP7

Answer Key

Unit 2: CORE Place Value, Multiplication, and Expression Concepts

Place Value

Page 19 Practice: Now you try

1. 10
2. $\frac{1}{10}$
3. 56
4. 950,000
5. Her younger sister has 40 songs.
6. 3,800 students

Ace It Time: Jackson is correct. The digit 5 in 500,000 is one place to the left compared to 50,000. Moving to the left one place is the same as multiplying by 10 (being 10 times greater).

Powers of Ten (Exponents)

Page 21 Practice: Now you try

1. 1600
2. 0.450
3. 28,000
4. 0.47
5. 45×10^4
6. 16×10^3

Ace It Time: Casey will spend $99.00 if she buys 10 songs at $0.99 each for 10 months. To solve, first multiply $0.99 × 10 to find out how much she spends on songs in one month. Then, multiply that amount by 10 again to find out how much she spends in 10 months. This is $0.99 × 10 × 10, which is the same as 0.99×10^2.

Multiplication Using Partial Products and Area Models

Page 23 Practice: Now you try

1. 3,325
2. 5,848
3. 4,088
4. 36,945

5. 2,520 words
6. 437 apps

Ace It Time: 235 × 13 = 3,055, so Marley made an error in her math. She did not regroup in the thousands place when adding the products (705 + 2,350).

Multiplication Using the Standard Algorithm

Page 25 Practice: Now you try

1. 2,128
2. 32,895
3. 76,175
4. 212,511

Ace It Time: The missing digit is a 7. 23 × 47 = 1,081. To solve, first solve to find that 23 × 40 = 920.

$$\begin{array}{r} 23 \\ \times\ 40 \\ \hline 920 \end{array}$$

To get to 1,081, the number in the ones digit has to end in a 1 when multiplied by 3. Test your multiplication facts:

$$1 \times 3 = 3$$
$$2 \times 3 = 6$$
$$3 \times 3 = 9$$
$$4 \times 3 = 12$$
$$5 \times 3 = 15$$
$$6 \times 3 = 18$$
$$7 \times 3 = 21$$
$$8 \times 3 = 24$$
$$9 \times 3 = 27$$
$$10 \times 3 = 30$$

Since the only number that gives a 1 in the ones place is 7, the missing digit is 7.

Expressions

Page 27 Practice: Now you try

1. 22   2. 27   3. 12
4. 15   5. 5

Ace It Time: The recipe will need 9 cups of ingredients in all. You can calculate the answer two ways:

You can triple the cups of flour (3 × 2) and then triple the cups of sugar (3 × 1). Add the cups of sugar and flower together to get the total cups of all ingredients: (3 × 2) + (3 × 1).

You can recognize that the original recipe required 2 cups of flour + 1 cup of sugar = 3 cups of ingredients, and then triple that amount: 3 × (2 + 1).

Writing Expressions

Page 28: Now you try

1. (14 – 5) + (3 × 2)
2. (144 ÷ 12) × 4 + 17
3. 4 – 4 + 2
4. 20 – (8 + 6) OR 20 – 8 – 6
5. (4 × 12) × 2 OR (4 × 12) + (4 × 12)
6. 52 – 6 – 6 OR 52 – (6 + 6) OR 52 – 6 × 2

Ace It Time: Mr. Young hiked (4 + 4) × 7. Mrs. Young hiked (4 × 2) × 7. These expressions are the same because (4 × 2) can also be written as (4 + 4). Mr. and Mrs. Young hiked the same amount.

Stop and Think! Review Unit 2

Page 30 Activity Section 1:

1. 10^2 OR 100
2. 10^3 OR 1,000
3. 10^2 OR 100
4. 10^3 OR 1,000
5. 10
6. 100
7. $\frac{1}{100}$
8. $\frac{1}{10}$

Page 31 Activity Section 2:

1. 2
2. 4
3. 2
4. 2
5. 520; 5,200; 52,000; 52×10^4; 520,000; 10×10×10×10×10; 10^5; 5,200,000

Activity Section 3:

1. 728 texts

2. 4,275 pounds

3. 6,072 cubes

4. 28,140 miles

Page 32 Activity Section 4:

1. 25,410

2. 132,204

3. 1,560 miles

4. 77,550 skateboards

5. 5,310 words

Activity Section 5:

1. $22 - (2 + 4) \times 2$

2. $48 \div 6 \times (15 - 12)$

3. $28 - 2 \times (3 + 6)$

4. $(5 + 3) \times 4 \div 2$

5. B

6. C

Page 33 Activity Section 6:

1. $(14 \times 4) - (6 \times 4)$ OR $4 \times (14 - 6)$

2. $12 \times 4 \div 2$

3. $60 - 18 + 15$

4. $5 \times 6 \times 2$

Stop and Think! Unit 2 Understand

Page 34 Activity Section: Beth and Corey have saved $(3 \times 2) \times 6$ dollars = $36. They will be able to buy the game when they have $45, which means they have $9 left to save. To find out how much more they have to save, subtract from $45: $45 - (3 \times 2) \times 6$.

Stop and Think! Unit 2 Discover

Page 35 Activity Section: The total number of seats in the theater will be the sum of the number of seats in each section.

The middle section has 24 rows of 20 seats, or $24 \times 20 = 480$ seats.

There are 2 side sections with 24 rows of 8 seats, or $2 \times 24 \times 8 = 384$ seats.

The back section has 8 rows of 32 seats, or $8 \times 32 = 256$ seats.

In total, there are $480 + 384 + 256 = 1{,}120$ seats.

Unit 3: CORE Division Concepts

Area Model Division

Page 37 Practice: Now you try

1. 591; $500 + 80 + 11 = 591$

2. Possible break apart:
   $(2{,}100 \div 3) + (72 \div 3)$, $700 + 24 = 724$

Ace It Time: Yes, he has enough money. Each box covers 8 square feet (1 square foot × 8 paving stones). He needs 24 boxes because $192 \div 8 = 24$. It will cost $24 \times \$10$ a box = $240. He has $400 saved and he only needs $240. That is $160 more.

Division with Partial Quotients

Page 39 Practice: Now you try

1. 139

2. 441

Ace It Time: Sebastian made an error in the third partial quotient, which changed the total quotient. He should have taken 4 groups of 3 out, not 1. The corrected work is shown in red below.

```
3    2232
   – 2100    3 × 700   2100
     132
   – 120    3 × 40    120
     12
   – 12    3 × 4     12
      0          Quotient: 2, 232
```

Standard Division with One-Digit Divisors

Page 41 Practice: Now you try

1. 1,514

2. 1,060

Ace It Time: Trey's first error is in the thousands place of the quotient. 2 (the divisor) can go into 5,000 twice, so there should be a 2 in the thousands place of the quotient. Trey also listed that 2 went into 32 16 times, and listed that as part of the quotient.

```
     2 6 1 2
  2 )5 2 2 4
    – 4
    ———
     1 2
    – 1 2
    ———
      0 2
     – 2
     ———
      0 4
      – 4
      ———
        0
```

Standard Division with Two-Digit Divisors

Page 43 Practice: Now you try

1. 145

2. 213

3. 247

Ace It Time: Bryce and his father can plant 48 rows with 39 seeds in each row because $1{,}872 \div 39 = 48$. I can check with multiplication $48 \times 39 = 1{,}872$.

Division with Remainders

Page 45 Practice: Now you try

1. 156 r4

2. 374 r17

3. 342 r8

Ace It Time: Each person will receive $14\frac{4}{8}$, or $14\frac{1}{2}$ pipe cleaners each because $116 \div 8 = 14 \text{ r}\frac{4}{8}$, or $14\frac{1}{2}$.

Interpreting Remainders

Page 47 Practice: Now you try

1. $339 \div 7 = 48 \text{ r}3$

   a. The 3 left over students would require a seat on another mini-van, making the total minivans needed 49.

   b. That minivan will only be holding the 3 leftover students.

2. $237 \div 19 = 12 \text{ r}9$

   a. There will be 12 full cottages.

   b. There will be 9 family members in the cottage that is not full.

Ace It Time: $2{,}467 \div 55 = 44 \text{ r}47$. Since 55 people can fit on one bus, they will need 44 FULL buses, PLUS one more bus for the 47 remaining students, so that is 45 buses in all.

Stop and Think! Unit 3 Review

Page 48 Activity Section 1:

1. 33 soccer balls

2. 67 songs

3. 469 ear buds

4. 209 calculators

Page 49 Activity Section 2:

1. 265

2. 217

3. 212

4. 81 r31

5. 374 r9

6. 124

7. $140

8. 127 screens

Page 50 Activity Section 3:

1. 24 cases

2. 11 characters, 5 coins leftover

3. $5\frac{18}{36}$, or $5\frac{1}{2}$ feet each

4. 3 buses in all

Stop and Think! Unit 3 Understand

Page 51 Activity Section: Timothy used the standard algorithm.

Chris used the area model.

Lori used partial quotients.

Wendy used partial quotients.

Possible answer: Student should explain which division method they prefer, and explain why (based on number sense, time it takes to solve, etc.)

Stop and Think! Unit 3 Discover

Page 52 Activity Section: Keisha is incorrect because
$115 \div 12 = 9$ r7. So she will have nine 12-inch pieces with $\frac{7}{12}$ inches of string leftover. (We can interpret this remainder as a fraction because string is something that we can have a "fraction of.") You can also tell she is incorrect by checking her answer with multiplication: Ten 12-inch pieces would be $10 \times 12 = 120$, and we only have 115 inches of string, so her answer is too high.

Unit 4: CORE Adding and Subtracting Decimals Concepts

Place Value in Decimals

Page 54 Practice: Now you try

1. 0.5 or five tenths

2. .008 or eight thousandths

3. $4 \times 10 + 4 \times 1 + 4 \times (\frac{1}{10}) + 4 \times (\frac{1}{100}) + 4 \times (\frac{1}{1000})$

4. $7 \times 100 + 1 \times 10 + 4 \times 1 + 6 \times (\frac{1}{10}) + 1 \times (\frac{1}{100}) + 9 \times (\frac{1}{1000})$

5. One and twenty five hundredths

6. Twelve and four hundred-six thousandths

7. 20.16

8. 472.923

Page 55 Ace It Time: Jack is correct. In 23.365, the digit 5 is in the thousandths place, so the decimal goes to the thousandths. Bailey looked at the decimal and considered it the same as 365 (three hundred and sixty-five), but decimals have different place values than whole numbers. A whole number with three places is in the hundreds, but a decimal with three places is in the thousandths.

Comparing and Ordering Decimals

Page 56 Practice: Now you try

1. 2.545, 2.554, 25.450

2. 20.155, 21.550, 21.551

3. 45.200, 45.230, 45.233

4. 0.114, 0.411, 0.414

Page 57

5. 51.551, 51.151, 51.115

6. 0.809, 0.808, 0.089

7. 0.200, 0.020, 0.002

8. 1.400, 1.040, 1.004

Ace It Time: It rained the most in the month of August, and the least in September. The inches listed from least to greatest are 6.638, 6.682, 7.070, 7.700.

Rounding Decimals

Page 59 Practice: Now you try

1. 23.6

2. 1.23

3. 0.1

4. 181.8

5. 10

6. 0.01

7. 18.13 gallons

8. $17.00

Ace It Time: 5.999 rounded to the nearest tenth is 6.0 because rounding up 9 tenths gives 10 tenths, which is equal to 1 whole.

Adding and Subtracting Decimals

Page 61 Practice: Now you try

1. 48.13

2. 2.23

3. 17.13 minutes

4. 49.74 pounds

Ace It Time: Together they have saved $36.20. They need to save $3.80 more, because $40.00 − 36.20 = 3.80.

Stop and Think! Unit 4 Review

Page 62 Activity Section 1:

1. $5 \times (\frac{1}{10}) + 6 \times (\frac{1}{100}) + 8 \times (\frac{1}{1000})$, five hundred sixty-eight thousandths

2. $1 \times 10 + 4 \times 1 + 7 \times (\frac{1}{10}) + 8 \times (\frac{1}{100})$, fourteen and seventy-eight hundredths

3. $4 \times 100 + 2 \times (\frac{1}{10}) + 5 \times (\frac{1}{100})$, four hundred and twenty-five tenths

4. $8 \times 100 + 9 \times 10 + 8 \times (\frac{1}{10}) + 9 \times (\frac{1}{1000})$, eight hundred ninety and eight hundred and nine thousandths

5. $7 \times 100 + 8 \times 1 + 2 \times (\frac{1}{100})$, seven hundred and eight and two hundredths

6. $9 \times 100 + 9 \times 10 + 9 \times 1 + 9 \times (\frac{1}{10}) + 9 \times (\frac{1}{100}) + 9 \times (\frac{1}{1000})$, nine hundred ninety-nine and nine hundred ninety-nine thousandths

Page 63 Activity Section 2:

1. <

2. >

3. =

4. <

5. <

6. >

7. 29.25, 29.03, 25.35, 23.5

Answer Key

8. 4.002, 4.202, 4.220, 4.222

9. Jim ran fastest because 2.7 < 2.75

Page 64 Activity Section 3:

1. 0.38

2. 69.0 pounds

3. 24.21 inches

4. 1.2 mL

5. 4.0 miles

Page 65 Activity Section 4:

1. 100.2 degrees

2. 6.39 miles

3. 3.37 pounds

4. $9,094.50 in all, $905.50 away from their goal

Stop and Think! Unit 4 Understand

Page 66 Possible Answers:

0.378

0.387

0.738

0.783

Sample explanation: I know this is ordered from least to greatest because I order the decimals from left to right, using the given numbers 0, 3, 7, and 8. Since the smallest number is 0, I can use that in the ones place. Then I can move to the next smallest number (3) and make 0.378, then 0.387, 0.738, 0.783, etc. Other possible answers: 3.078, 3.087, 7.038, 7.308, etc.

Stop and Think! Unit 4 Discover

Page 67 Activity Section: These three decimals round to 4.5: 4.53, because the 3 in the hundredths is less than five.

4.48, because the 8 in the hundredths place is greater than five.

4.452, because the 2 in the thousandths place is less than five.

Any decimals between 4.45-4.54 and 4.501-4.549 would round to 4.5 when rounded to the nearest tenth.

Unit 5: CORE Multiplying and Dividing Decimals Concepts

Multiplication Patterns with Decimals
Page 69 Practice: Now you try

1. 7.15, 71.5, 715.0, 7,150.0

2. 13.45, 134.5, 1,345, 13,450

3. 6,124, 612.4, 61.24, 6.124

Ace It Time: Kendra is incorrect because $1.55 \times 1,000 = 1,550$.

Multiplying Decimals and Whole Numbers
Page 71 Practice: Now you try

1. 30.17

2. 18.8

3. 12.78

4. 6.20

Ace It Time: Jeanine spends $8.97 in grapes because $2.99 \times 3 = 8.97$. Mark spends $6.98 in grapes because $3.49 \times 2 = 6.98$. Mark spent $1.99 less because $8.97 – $6.98 = $1.99.

Multiplying Decimals
Page 73 Practice: Now you try

1. 1.35

2. 15.12

3. 37.96

4. 30.044

5. 3.375 hours

6. $21.25

Ace It Time: Taka is correct because $4.5 \times 0.4 = 1.8$. Pele put the decimal point in the wrong place.

Division Patterns with Decimals
Page 75 Practice: Now you try

1. 242, 24.2, 2.42, 0.242

2. 38, 3.8, 0.38, 0.038

3. 146, 14.6, 1.46, 0.146

4. 11, 1.1, 0.11, 0.011

Ace It Time: Ella is correct. $15 \div 101 = 1.5$, and $15 \times 0.1 = 1.5$. They are both breaking 15 into one tenth.

Dividing Decimals and Whole Numbers
Page 77 Practice: Now you try

1. 0.56

2. 1.38

3. 0.36

4. 1.25

Ace It Time: It costs $12.65 for each friend to bowl because $50.60 ÷ 4 friends = $12.65. (Remember that Leah and her 3 friends is a total of 4 people.)

Dividing Decimals
Page 79 Practice: Now you try

1. 7.0

2. 3.5

3. 0.2

4. 8.0

Ace It Time: Calvin will have 20 dimes because $2.00 \div 0.10 = 20$. You can write a dime as $0.10.

Stop and Think! Unit 5 Review

Page 80 Activity Section 1:

1. 2.6, 26, 260, 2,600

2. 56, 5.6, 0.56

3. 23.88, 238.8, 2,388, 23,880

4. 4,450 inches

Activity Section 2:

1. 19.6

2. 220.9

3. 271.70

4. 726 miles

Page 81 Activity Section 3:

1. 8.36

2. 9.45

3. 2.16

4. 8.0 feet tall

Activity Section 4:

1. 556, 55.6, 5.56, 0.556

2. 88.8, 8.88, 0.888

3. 405, 40.5, 4.05, 0.405

4. 4.25 pounds per loaf

Page 82 Activity Section 5:

1. 0.80

2. 0.81

3. 16.1

4. $10.70 each

Activity Section 6:

1. 9

2. 800

3. 81

4. 9 family members

Stop and Think! Unit 5 Understand
Page 83 Frankie spent $34.40 because $8.60 \times 4 = 34.40$.

Craig spent 34.40 + 5.88, or $40.28. "Times as much" tells us to multiply and "more than" tells us to add.

Stop and Think! Unit 5 Discover

Page 84 Each notebook cost $1.25. First, subtract the tax from the total, so $27.79 − $1.82 tax = $25.97.

Next, she spent $20.97 on 3 books at $6.99 each, because 6.99 × 3 = 20.97. So subtract that amount: (25.97 − 20.97 = 5.00). $5.00÷4 notebooks = $1.25 per notebook.

Unit 6: CORE Adding and Subtracting Fractions Concepts

Adding and Subtracting Fractions with Unlike Denominators

Page 87 Practice: Now you try

1. $\frac{7}{20}$
2. $\frac{4}{5}$
3. $\frac{1}{3}$
4. $\frac{1}{2}$

Ace It Time: Mario had $\frac{1}{12}$ cup of mix left. First he made $\frac{1}{3} + \frac{1}{4} = \frac{7}{12}$ cups of trail mix. Then he gave $\frac{1}{2}$ cup to his brother. $\frac{7}{12} - \frac{1}{2} = \frac{1}{12}$ cup.

The Common Denominator

Page 89 Practice: Now you try

1. $\frac{5}{8}$
2. $\frac{1}{4}$
3. $\frac{1}{6}$

Ace It Time: Jackson has $\frac{1}{2}$ meter of twine left after making one bracelet because $\frac{4}{5} - \frac{3}{10} = \frac{8}{10} - \frac{3}{10} = \frac{5}{10} = \frac{1}{2}$. Jackson can make two bracelets because $\frac{4}{5} - \frac{3}{10} - \frac{3}{10} = \frac{8}{10} - \frac{3}{10} - \frac{3}{10} = \frac{2}{10}$. Since $\frac{2}{10} < \frac{3}{10}$, he doesn't have enough twine to make a third bracelet.

Adding and Subtracting Mixed Numbers

Page 91 Practice: Now you try

1. $12\frac{11}{12}$
2. $1\frac{1}{10}$
3. $3\frac{3}{5}$
4. $2\frac{1}{4}$

Ace It Time: Zea walked $2\frac{3}{8} + \frac{3}{4} = 2\frac{9}{8} = 3\frac{1}{8}$ miles. Gabe walked $2\frac{3}{8} + \frac{7}{8} = 2\frac{10}{8} = 3\frac{2}{8} = 3\frac{1}{4}$ miles. Zea is wrong because $3\frac{1}{4} > 3\frac{1}{8}$. Gabe walked $\frac{1}{8}$ mile more than Zea because $3\frac{1}{4} - 3\frac{1}{8} = \frac{1}{8}$ mile.

Subtracting Mixed Numbers with Regrouping

Page 93 Practice: Now you try

1. $1\frac{7}{10}$
2. $4\frac{7}{9}$
3. $6\frac{1}{3}$
4. $5\frac{7}{12}$

Ace It Time: Carla regrouped $8\frac{6}{12}$ incorrectly. Performing the subtraction shows this:

First, she found the common denominator (12) and found the equivalent fractions $8\frac{2}{4} = 8\frac{6}{12}$. She realized $2\frac{4}{6} = 2\frac{8}{12}$. But she made an error by treating the top number like it was $\frac{16}{12}$. She added a 10 to the numerator instead of adding $\frac{12}{12}$.

$$\begin{array}{r} \overset{7}{\cancel{8}}\overset{16}{\cancel{\frac{6}{12}}} \\ -\ 2\frac{8}{12} \\ \hline 5\frac{8}{12} \end{array}$$

Right way:

$$8\frac{2}{4} \longrightarrow 8\frac{6}{12} \longrightarrow 7\frac{18}{12}$$
$$-2\frac{4}{6} \longrightarrow 2\frac{8}{12} \qquad -2\frac{8}{12}$$

Correct Answer: $5\frac{10}{12}$

Stop and Think! Unit 6 Review

Page 94 Activity Section 1:

1. $1\frac{1}{8}$
2. $1\frac{1}{3}$
3. $\frac{10}{9}$, or $1\frac{1}{9}$
4. $\frac{3}{10}$
5. $\frac{2}{6}$, or $\frac{1}{3}$
6. $\frac{7}{10}$
7. $\frac{5}{8}$ more
8. $\frac{14}{12}$, or $1\frac{2}{12}$, or $1\frac{1}{6}$ hours, or 1 hour and 10 minutes. ($\frac{2}{4}$ of an hour is 30 min, $\frac{2}{3}$ of an hour is 40 minutes, so that is 70 minutes, or 1 hour and 10 minutes in all.)

Page 95 Activity Section 2:

1. $\frac{3}{5} = \frac{6}{10}, \frac{4}{10} = \frac{4}{10}$
2. $\frac{3}{6} = \frac{6}{12}, \frac{4}{12} = \frac{4}{12}$
3. $\frac{8}{9} = \frac{8}{9}, \frac{2}{3} = \frac{6}{9}$
4. $\frac{10}{9}$, or $1\frac{1}{9}$
5. $\frac{3}{8}$
6. $\frac{38}{30}$, or $1\frac{8}{30}$, or $1\frac{4}{15}$
7. $\frac{3}{4}$ pound of paper
8. $\frac{2}{6}$, or $\frac{1}{3}$ of a bar

Page 96 Activity Section 3:

1. $1\frac{4}{8}$, or $1\frac{1}{2}$ miles
2. $4\frac{1}{6}$ pounds
3. $12\frac{17}{12}$, or $13\frac{5}{12}$ feet of rope
4. $10\frac{7}{6}$, or $11\frac{1}{6}$ feet of yarn
5. $5\frac{1}{6}$ feet
6. $9\frac{5}{8}$ cups

Page 97 Activity Section 4:

1. $1\frac{4}{6}$, or $1\frac{2}{3}$
2. $4\frac{5}{6}$
3. $\frac{7}{8}$
4. $1\frac{13}{14}$
5. $5\frac{5}{6}$ inches

Answer Key

Stop and Think! Unit 6 Understand

Page 98 Activity Section: Jorge can bring the three bags with the following weights:

$7\frac{5}{8}$ pounds, $8\frac{1}{4}$ pounds, and $8\frac{7}{8}$ pounds. ($7\frac{5}{8} + 8\frac{1}{4} + 8\frac{7}{8} = 24\frac{3}{4}$ pound)

If he brings the bag that weighs $15\frac{1}{2}$ pounds, he will only be able to bring two bags because $15\frac{1}{2}$ plus any of the other weights is almost 25 pounds.

Stop and Think! Unit 6 Discover

Page 99 Activity Section:

1. $2\frac{5}{12}$ in.
2. $3\frac{3}{4}$ in.
3. $6\frac{1}{6}$ in. (or $2\frac{5}{12} + 3\frac{3}{4} = 5\frac{14}{12} = 6\frac{1}{6}$)
4. $\frac{5}{6}$ in.
5. $\frac{1}{2}$ in.

Unit 7: CORE Multiplying Fractions Concepts

Fractional Parts

Page 101 Practice: Now you try

1. 6
2. 8
3. 9
4. 12

Ace It Time: There are 16 cats and 24 dogs. $\frac{2}{5} \times 40 = 16$ cats. $\frac{3}{5} \times 40 = 24$ dogs. You can check this by adding. 16 cats + 24 dogs = 40 pets.

Making Sense of Fractions, Factors, and Products

Page 103 Practice: Now you try

1. equal to
2. greater than
3. less than
4. less than
5. equal to
6. greater than

Ace It Time: Emily is right. Carlito may have been thinking that $\frac{2}{3} > \frac{1}{4}$, so the product must be greater. However, both $\frac{1}{4}$ and $\frac{2}{3}$ are less than 1. When multiplying by a number less than 1, the product is less than the original number.

Multiplying Fractions and Whole Numbers

Page 105 Practice: Now you try

1. 2
2. 3
3. $1\frac{2}{3}$
4. $\frac{3}{4}$
5. $1\frac{3}{4}$ miles
6. 6 games

Ace It Time: Answers will vary, but you should have the whole number 5 × any fractional part in fifths. The multiplication problems can be the same, just written two ways to show the Commutative Property of Multiplication.

For example: $5 \times \frac{2}{5}$ and $\frac{2}{5} \times 5$.

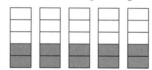

$\frac{1}{4} \times \frac{2}{3}$ is less than $\frac{1}{4}$.

$\frac{2}{3} \times \frac{1}{4}$ is less than $\frac{2}{3}$.

Multiplying Fractions

Page 107 Practice: Now you try

1. $\frac{1}{8}$
2. $\frac{1}{6}$
3. $\frac{1}{3}$
4. $\frac{1}{5}$
5. $\frac{5}{8}$ of the class are girls with brown eyes
6. $\frac{1}{4}$ inch of water evaporated

Ace It Time: Jon eats 2 slices of pizza. After Jim eats $\frac{1}{3}$ of the pizza, $\frac{2}{3}$ is left. Jon eats $\frac{1}{4}$ of what's left. That is $\frac{1}{4}$ of $\frac{2}{3}$ of the pizza. $\frac{1}{4} \times \frac{2}{3} = \frac{2}{12} = \frac{1}{6}$ of the pizza. $\frac{1}{6}$ of 12 slices = 2 slices.

You can also think about this as whole slices multiplied by a fraction. After Jim eats his slices, there are 12 − 4 = 8 slices left. Jon eats $\frac{1}{4}$ of those slices. $\frac{1}{4} \times 8$ slices = $\frac{8}{4}$ = 2 slices.

Area and Mixed Numbers

Page 109 Practice: Now you try

1. $1\frac{7}{8}$
2. $2\frac{2}{9}$
3. $7\frac{1}{3}$ square feet
4. $4\frac{3}{8}$ square feet

Ace It Time: The area of the floor is $3\frac{1}{2} \times 5\frac{3}{4} = 20\frac{1}{8}$ square feet.

Multiplication with Mixed Numbers

Page 111 Practice: Now you try

1. $5\frac{1}{8}$ pounds
2. 40 feet
3. $6\frac{3}{4}$ miles
4. $8\frac{13}{15}$ square feet

Ace It Time: You will need $5\frac{3}{4} \times 1\frac{1}{2} = 8\frac{5}{8}$ cups of fruit punch.

You can solve with the Distributive Property or by other methods.

Distributive Property:

$$5\frac{3}{4} \times 1\frac{1}{2} = (5 + \frac{3}{4}) \times (1 + \frac{1}{2})$$
$$= 5 \times (1 + \frac{1}{2}) + \frac{3}{4}(1 + \frac{1}{2})$$
$$= (5 \times 1) + (5 \times \frac{1}{2}) + (\frac{3}{4} \times 1) + (\frac{3}{4} \times \frac{1}{2})$$
$$= 5 + \frac{5}{2} + \frac{3}{4} + \frac{3}{8}$$
$$= 5 + 2\frac{1}{2} + \frac{3}{4} + \frac{3}{8}$$
$$= 5 + 2\frac{4}{8} + \frac{6}{8} + \frac{3}{8}$$
$$= 8\frac{5}{8}$$

Stop and Think! Unit 7 Review

Page 112 Activity Section 1:

1. 15
2. 28
3. 12
4. 8 are red and 16 are yellow
5. 12 apps are for school and 24 are for fun

Page 113 Activity Section 2:

1. less than
2. less than
3. less than
4. greater than
5. The first flower bed is larger because $\frac{7}{8}$ is greater than $\frac{4}{6}$. This means

$4 \times \frac{7}{8}$ will be larger than $4 \times \frac{4}{6}$. Both are smaller than 4 square feet because multiplying 4 by a fraction means the product is less than 4.

6. $8,450 \times \frac{3}{4}$. So far they have sold less food than last year.

Activity Section 3:

1. $\frac{4}{6} \times 6 = 4$ Student should draw 6 rectangles, each rectangle broken into sixths, and 4 sixths shaded in each rectangle.

2. $\frac{1}{5} \times 3 = \frac{3}{5}$ Student should draw a number line labeled 0, $\frac{1}{5}$, $\frac{2}{5}$, $\frac{3}{5}$, etc. Show arrows to make three $\frac{1}{5}$ hops.

3. $4 \times \frac{2}{3} = 2\frac{2}{3}$ Student should draw 4 rectangles broken into thirds, with 2 thirds shaded in each rectangle. Student should draw a number line broken into thirds, with 4 hops of $\frac{2}{3}$ each to end at $2\frac{2}{3}$.

4. $\frac{3}{4}$ roll

5. 4 pounds

Page 114 Activity Section 4:

1. $\frac{3}{8}$

2. $\frac{1}{6}$

3. $\frac{2}{7}$

4. $\frac{1}{4}$ cup of shredded zucchini

5. $\frac{1}{2}$ pound of turkey

Activity Section 5:

1.

	2	$\frac{1}{4}$
1	1×2	$1 \times \frac{1}{4}$
$\frac{1}{4}$	$\frac{1}{4} \times 2$	$\frac{1}{4} \times \frac{1}{4}$

$2 \times 1 = 2$
$1 \times \frac{1}{4} = \frac{1}{4}$
$\frac{1}{4} \times 2 = \frac{2}{4}$
$\frac{1}{4} \times \frac{1}{4} = \frac{1}{16}$
Answer: $2\frac{13}{16}$

2.

	4	$\frac{5}{6}$
2	2×4	$2 \times \frac{5}{6}$
$\frac{2}{3}$	$\frac{2}{3} \times 4$	$\frac{2}{3} \times \frac{5}{6}$

$2 \times 4 = 8$
$2 \times \frac{5}{6} = \frac{10}{6} = 1\frac{2}{3}$
$\frac{2}{3} \times 4 = \frac{8}{3} = 2\frac{2}{3}$
$\frac{2}{3} \times \frac{5}{6} = \frac{10}{18} = \frac{5}{9}$
Answer: $12\frac{8}{9}$

3. $3\frac{1}{4} \times 2\frac{2}{8} = 7\frac{5}{16}$ square meters

Page 115 Activity Section 6:

1. $4\frac{13}{16}$ miles

2. $9\frac{11}{16}$ miles

3. $4\frac{3}{8}$ bins

Stop and Think! Unit 7 Understand

Page 116 Rosa and Tessa rode bikes together for $\frac{1}{2} \times \frac{1}{2} = \frac{1}{4}$ of an hour. This is equal to 15 minutes. There are 60 minutes in an hour. $\frac{1}{4} \times 60 = 15$ minutes.

Stop and Think! Unit 7 Discover

Page 117 The backyard is $148\frac{1}{2}$ square feet. The patio is $10\frac{1}{2} \times 5\frac{3}{4} = 60\frac{3}{8}$ square feet. This means that $148\frac{1}{2} - 60\frac{3}{8} = 88\frac{1}{8}$ square feet of their yard is NOT part of the patio. The answer is $88\frac{1}{8}$ square feet.

Unit 8: CORE Dividing Fractions Concepts

Dividing Fractions and Whole Numbers

Page 119 Practice: Now you try

1. $3 \div \frac{1}{6} = 18$; $18 \times \frac{1}{6} = 3$

2. $\frac{1}{4} \div 3 = \frac{1}{12}$; $\frac{1}{12} \times 3 = \frac{1}{4}$

3. $4 \div \frac{1}{4} = 16$; $16 \times \frac{1}{4} = 4$

4. 8 times

Ace It Time: Morgan spent $\frac{1}{4}$ of an hour on each assignment. $\frac{3}{4} \div 3 = \frac{1}{4}$ hour. You can find this answer in minutes. There are 60 minutes in an hour. $\frac{1}{4} \times 60 = 15$ minutes. Morgan spent 15 minutes on each assignment.

Using Models to Divide Fractions and Whole Numbers

Page 121 Practice: Now you try

1. $\frac{1}{5} \div 4 = \frac{1}{20}$; $\frac{1}{20} \times 4 = \frac{1}{5}$

2. $3 \div \frac{1}{5} = 15$; $15 \times \frac{1}{5} = 3$

3. $\frac{1}{5} \div 5 = \frac{1}{25}$; $\frac{1}{25} \times 5 = \frac{1}{5}$

4. $9 \div \frac{1}{2} = 18$; $18 \times \frac{1}{2} = 9$

5. 60 members

Ace It Time: It would take the tortoise 30 seconds to travel 10 feet.

$10 \div \frac{1}{3} = 30$

Interpreting Fractions as Division

Page 123 Practice: Now you try

1. $\frac{5}{4} = 1\frac{1}{4}$

2. $\frac{3}{6} = \frac{1}{2}$

3. $\frac{9}{5} = 1\frac{4}{5}$

4. $\frac{6}{8} = \frac{3}{4}$

Ace It Time: There are 35 index cards divided by 15 members.

$\frac{35}{15} = 2\frac{1}{3}$ cards for each member.

Stop and Think! Unit 8 Review

Page 124 Activity Section 1:

1. $\frac{1}{10}$

2. 12

3. $\frac{1}{24}$

4. 100

5. $\frac{1}{20}$

6. 30

7. $3 \div \frac{1}{4} = 12$ quarters

8. $8 \div \frac{1}{4} = 32$ people

9. $5 \div \frac{1}{4} = 20$ projects

10. $\frac{1}{2} \div 4 = \frac{1}{8}$ piece of paper

11. $\frac{1}{2} \div 3 = \frac{1}{6}$ stick of butter

Page 125 Activity Section 2:

1. $\frac{1}{7} \div 2 = \frac{1}{14}$; $\frac{1}{14} \times 2 = \frac{1}{7}$

2. $24 \div \frac{1}{2} = 48$; $48 \times \frac{1}{2} = 24$

3. $\frac{1}{2} \div 5 = \frac{1}{10}$; $\frac{1}{10} \times 5 = \frac{1}{2}$

4. $\frac{1}{4} \div 8 = \frac{1}{32}$; $\frac{1}{32} \times 8 = \frac{1}{4}$

5. $4 \div \frac{1}{9} = 36$; $36 \times \frac{1}{9} = 4$

6. $\frac{1}{3} \div 10 = \frac{1}{30}$; $\frac{1}{30} \times 10 = \frac{1}{3}$

7. $\frac{1}{2} \div 2 = \frac{1}{4}$ of a watermelon

8. $6 \div \frac{1}{3} = 18$ pieces of fabric

9. $2 \div \frac{1}{4} = 8$ times

Activity Section 3:

1. $3 \div 6 = \frac{3}{6} = \frac{1}{2}$

2. $4 \div 5 = \frac{4}{5}$

3. $10 \div 12 = \frac{10}{12} = \frac{5}{6}$

4. $\frac{7}{4} = 1\frac{3}{4}$

5. $\frac{2}{8} = \frac{1}{4}$

6. $\frac{12}{7} = 1\frac{5}{7}$

7. $3 \div 5 = \frac{3}{5}$ of the bar

8. $13 \div 4 = \frac{13}{4} = 3\frac{1}{4}$ muffins

Stop and Think! Unit 8 Understand

Page 126 Activity Section: She had 2 pans of brownies divided into eighths: $2 \div \frac{1}{8} = 16$ brownies.

If every person had 2 brownies, there were $16 \div 2 = 8$ people there.

Stop and Think! Unit 8 Discover

Page 127 Activity Section: The Math and Science Club is giving $3 \div 5 = \frac{3}{5}$ pints of ice cream to each student. The Student Council is giving $5 \div 8 = \frac{5}{8}$ pints of ice cream to each student. The Student Council is giving more ice cream to each student because $\frac{5}{8} = \frac{25}{40}$ is greater than $\frac{3}{5} = \frac{24}{40}$. Nima is right!

Unit 9: CORE Graphing and Algebraic Pattern Concepts

Line Plots

Page 129 Practice: Now you try

1. The animal shelter most often served $\frac{3}{8}$ cups of dog food. In total, they served $\frac{3}{8} + \frac{3}{8} + \frac{3}{8} + \frac{3}{8} = 1\frac{1}{2}$ cups of food with this serving size.

2. $\frac{5}{8} - \frac{1}{4} = \frac{3}{8}$ cup

3. 5 dogs received $\frac{1}{2}$ cup serving size or more: 3 received $\frac{1}{2}$ cup and 2 received $\frac{5}{8}$ cup.

4. The total amount of dog food served was $\frac{1}{4} + \frac{1}{4} + \frac{1}{4} + \frac{3}{8} + \frac{3}{8} + \frac{3}{8} + \frac{3}{8} + \frac{1}{2} + \frac{1}{2} + \frac{1}{2} + \frac{5}{8} + \frac{5}{8} = 5$ cups. There are 12 servings in total, so the average is 5 cups $\div 12 = \frac{5}{12}$ cup.

Ace It Time:

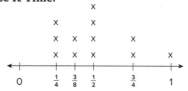

1. The total weight of the dwarf hamsters in the pet store is:
$(3 \times \frac{1}{4}) + (2 \times \frac{3}{8}) + (4 \times \frac{1}{2}) + (2 \times \frac{3}{4}) + \frac{8}{8} = 6$ pounds

2. The average weight of the dwarf hamsters is $6 \div 12 = \frac{1}{2}$ pound.

Ordered Pairs and Coordinate Planes

Page 130 Practice: Now you try

#1–8: See grid

9. The movie theater is 3 units to the right and 3 units down from her house.

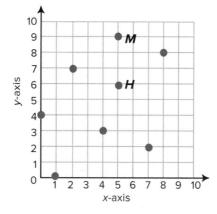

Ace It Time: The shape is an octagon because it has eight sides and eight points.

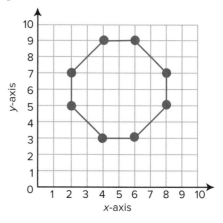

Line Graphs

Page 133 Practice: Now you try

1. (1,2) (3,4) (6,7) (9,7)

Growth of Plant

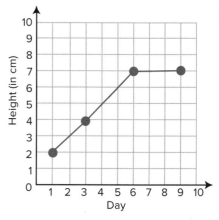

Sample Statement: The plant's height increased between Day 1 and Day 6. The plant stopped growing at Day 6.

Ace It Time: Money Saved

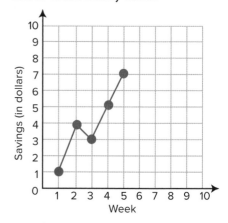

Note: You may choose to use a different interval for the x-axis, or only show weeks 1-5.

Sample statement: Nina saves a different amount of money each week. She saves the greatest amount of money on Week 5 ($8) and the least amount on Week 1 ($2.)

Identifying Numerical Patterns

Page 135 Practice: Now you try

1. Multiply the number of books by 8 to find the total spent.

Books	1	2	3	4
Total Spent	8	16	24	32

2. Divide the number of eggs by 2 to find the number of omelets.

Eggs	2	4	6	8
Omelets	1	2	3	4

Ace It Time:

1. Level 10: 40 coins and 20 lives

2. (4,2), (8,4), (12,6), (16,8), (20,10)

3. Multiply the number of the level by 4 to get the number of coins. Multiply the number of the level by 2 to get the number of lives. You can also divide the number of coins by 2 to get the number of lives.

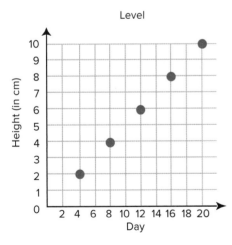

4. Answer should reflect that you looked at the relationship between the number of levels/coins, as well as the number of levels/lives. There is also a relationship between number of coins and lives. Answers

may also mention that the line graph is straight with no changes, which means there is a pattern.

Stop and Think! Unit 9 Review

Page 136 Activity Section 1:

1. 12 days

2. 21 quarts

3. $2\frac{1}{4} - 1\frac{1}{4} = 1$ quart

4. $21 \div 12 = 1\frac{3}{4}$ quarts

5. 7 days

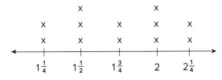

Page 137 Activity Section 2:

1. School: (4,1)
   Park: (7,3)
   Soccer Field: (5,7)
   Home: (2,9)

2. 6 blocks (2 blocks down, 3 blocks right)

3. See grid

4. (2,5) see grid

5. (8,7); 4 blocks away from the soccer field

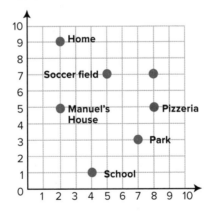

Page 138 Activity Section 3:

1. a, c, d, f

2. b - The number of phone calls Christina received decreased most from Day 5 to Day 6.
   e - The most phone calls Christina received in one day was 11.

3. Answers may vary, but should be similar to "Christina's Phone Calls."

Page 139 Activity Section 4:

1. Number of songs: 10; Amount of Money: $20

2. The amount of money is two times the number of songs.

3. (2,4) (4,8) (6,12) (8,16) (10,20)

4. Graph ordered pairs on coordinate grid.

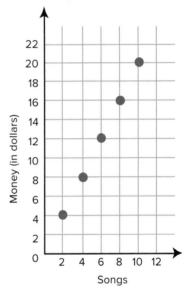

Music Downloads

Stop and Think! Unit 9 Understand

Page 140 Activity Section:

1.

Antwon's Pattern	
Term	Number
1	5
2	6
3	7
4	8
Antwon's rule: add 4	

Cole's Pattern	
Term	Number
1	4
2	6
3	8
4	10
Cole's rule: add 1, and multiply by 2	

2. Antwon's: (1,5) (2,6) (3,7) (4,8)
Cole's: (1,4) (2,6) (3,8) (4,10)

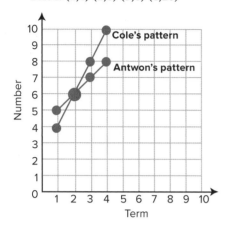

Stop and Think! Unit 9 Discover

Page 141

Ordered Pairs:

(1,2)

(2,4)

(3,5)

(4,4)

(5,4)

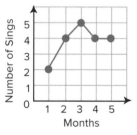

Chantell's Song Downloads

Statements: Statements will vary, but should be about how the data increases or decreases over the months. It may also include how the data stays the same (or she downloads the same amount of music) in Months 4 and 5. Month 3 had the greatest number of songs downloaded.

Unit 10: CORE Converting Units of Measurement Concepts

Customary Units of Length and Weight

Page 143 Practice: Now you try

1. 48 inches
2. 2 yards
3. 10,560 feet

4. 6 yards
5. 1 mile
6. 5 feet
7. 83 ounces
8. 6,000 pounds
9. >
10. <
11. =
12. >
13. <
14. >

Ace It Time: Mrs. Baker's classroom is longer. 32 feet = 10 yards and 2 feet. 10 yd. 2 ft. > 9 yd. 6 in.

Customary Units of Capacity

Page 145 Practice: Now you try

1. 2 pints
2. 12 quarts
3. 3 pints
4. 32 cups
5. 2 gallons
6. 2 cups
7. 8 pints
8. 72 pints
9. =
10. <
11. <

Ace It Time: Martez's sister sold more lemonade. Martez sold 8 quarts = 2 gallons. His sister sold 3 gallons, which is one more than 2 gallons.

Metric Units of Length and Weight

Page 147 Practice: Now you try

1. 1 gram
2. 40 mm
3. 0.350 km
4. 8,000 m
5. 26,000 m
6. 4.50 m
7. 1.2 cm
8. 3,500 g

Ace It Time: Micah's puppy weighs 5 kilograms. 1,000 g = 1 kg so 5,000 g = 5 kg. Since you are converting from smaller to larger, you divide. This moves the decimal point 3 spaces left.

Metric Units of Capacity

Page 149 Practice: Now you try

1. 16,000 mL

2. 425 daL
3. 0.050 mL
4. 0.8 hL
5. >
6. =
7. >

Ace It Time: 750 mL= 0.75 L, which is less than 7.5 L. So Ashanti collected less than 7.5 liters.

Elapsed Time

Page 151 Practice: Now you try

1. 5 hr 10 min
2. 255 min
3. 2 d 4 hr
4. 5 yr
5. 4 wk 2 d
6. 42 d

Ace It Time: The playlist ended at 12:55 p.m. 85 minutes = 1 hour 25 minutes. 1 hour and 25 minutes after 11:30 a.m. is 12:55 p.m.

Stop and Think! Unit 10 Review

Page 152 Activity Section 1:

1. Katy jumped farther. Jade jumped 108 inches = 9 feet = 3 yards. 3.5 yards > 3 yards.

2. Mr. Cohen needs 11 ft. 5 in. to complete the project. 65 in. = 5 ft. 5 in. 6 ft. + 5 ft. 5 in. = 11 ft. 5 in.

3. 40 tons

4. 102 feet

5. Kara's cat weighs more. 192 ounces = 12 pounds. 13 lbs > 12 lbs

Page 153 Activity Section 2:

1. 8C
2. 8 pints, 16 pints, 24 pints
3. 11 quarts
4. 1 cup
5. 6 quarts

Page 154 Activity Section 3:

1. 8500 m
2. Nate's flew farther. 3.5 m = 35 dm 40 dm > 35 dm
3. 320 mm
4. 42 mm = 4.2 cm 4.2 cm + 24 cm = 28.2 cm
5. 1,340 g

Page 155 Activity Section 4:

1. 2,000 mL
2. It is less than 250 cL.
   3 x 25 mL = 75 mL = 7.5 cL.
   7.5 cL < 250 cL.
3. 23.6 cL
4. 40,000 L
5. 45.8 daL

Page 156 Activity Section 5:

1. 720 seconds
2. 9:55 a.m.
3. 95 minutes
4. 12:55 p.m.
5. 9:30 a.m.

Stop and Think! Unit 10 Understand

Page 157 Activity Section: Each presentation takes 15 minutes + 5 minutes to clean up = 20 minutes. If there are 4 presentations, it takes 4 × 20 = 80 minutes = 1 hour 20 minutes for all of the presentations. They will finish at 6:50 p.m.

Stop and Think! Unit 10 Discover

Page 158 Activity Section: Each practice Landon sprints 5 × 20 = 100 yards. There are 1,760 yards in one mile.

It will take 1760 ÷ 100 = 17.6 practices to run one mile. This means it will take 17.6 × 2 = 35.2 practices to sprint a total of 2 miles. This means Landon is wrong. 35.2 practices > 20 practices.

Unit 11: CORE Geometry and Volume Concepts

Classifying Two-Dimensional Figures

Page 160 Practice: Now you try

1. False. A trapezoid has one pair of parallel sides.
2. False. Some rhombi are rectangles, but not all are. A rhombus does not need to have perpendicular sides.
3. False. A parallelogram does not need to have 4 equal sides. Opposite sides in a parallelogram need to be equal and parallel.
4. True
5. True -It has four right angles.
6. False. Some rectangles are squares, but not all are. A rectangle does not

need to have 4 congruent sides like a square.

7. False. Perpendicular lines meet and create a 90 degree angle.
8. False. A parallelogram has 2 sets of parallel sides.

Ace It Time: Isaac is not correct because all rhombi cannot be squares. A rhombus has 4 congruent sides like a square, but it does not have to have 4 right angles like a square. Izzy is correct. A square is a rhombus with 4 right angles.

Exploring Volume

Page 162 Practice: Now you try

1. 24 units^3
2. 75 units^3
3. 108 feet^3
4. 60 inches^3
5. 27 units^3
6. 48 units^3

Ace It Time: Sal is correct. Both towers have a volume of 12 cubic units. They are both made of 12 unit cubes. The difference is how the cubes are arranged.

Apply Formulas to Find Volume

Page 165 Practice: Now you try

1. 18 m^3
2. 96 ft^3

Ace It Time: Student drawings will vary but should show an example of how to stack the two rectangular prisms (or rice boxes) together to create a new structure. The total volume can be found by finding the volume of each prism.

8 × 8 × 2 = 128 in^3

2 × 4 × 6 = 48 in^3

128 + 48 = 176 in^3

Stop and Think! Unit 11 Review

Page 166 Activity Section 1:

1. quadrilateral, trapezoid
2. quadrilateral, rhombus, parallelogram
3. quadrilateral, square, rhombus, parallelogram, rectangle
4. quadrilateral, parallelogram
5. always; sometimes; always; sometimes; never; sometimes

Page 167 Activity Section 2:

1. 7 > 6
2. 60 > 50
3. 10 < 27
4. 36 < 48

Activity Section 3:

1. 6 ft.^{3}
2. 48 ft.^{3}
3. Yes, the box is big enough. The volume of the gaming system is 192 cubic inches, which is less than 200 cubic inches.
4. The crate is 2 feet tall because 12 ÷ 3 ÷ 2 = 2.
5. Measurements of prism #1 and #2 will vary depending on where you break apart the figure, but the total volume of the figure is 75 cubic yards.
6. Measurements of prism #1 and #2 will vary depending on where you break apart the figure, but the total volume of the figure is 184 cubic inches.

Stop and Think! Unit 11 Understand

Page 169 Activity Section:

Length	Width	Height	Volume
3 in.	4 in.	2 in.	24 cubic in.
1 ft.	5 ft.	3 ft.	15 cubic ft.
4 m	3 m	2 m	24 m^3
4 yd	6 yd	2 yd	48 cubic yd
6 cm	3 cm	4 cm	72 cm^3
6 ft.	2 ft.	3 ft.	36 cubic ft.
5 yd	3 yd	3 yd	45 yd^3

For the last two, answers will vary, but when multiplied together the factors should have a product of 36 ft^3 (example = 6 x 2 x 3) and 45 yd^3 (example = 5 x 3 x 3).

Explanations should reference multiplication to find volume and division to do the opposite.

Stop and Think! Unit 11 Discover

Page 170 Activity Section:

1. 112 inches^3
2. 128 inches^3
3. 240 inches^3

Customary Units Charts

Length
12 in. = 1 ft.
3 ft. = 1 yd
5,280 ft. = 1 mi
1,760 yd = 1 mi

Weight
16 oz = 1 lb
1 ton = 2,000 lb

Capacity
128 fl. oz = 1 gal
2 pt = 1 qt
8 pt = 1 gal
4 qt = 1 gal

Time
60 sec. = 1 min.
60 min. = 1 hr.
24 hr. = 1 day
7 days = 1 wk.
52 wk. = 1 yr.
12 mon. = 1 yr.
365 days = 1 yr
10 years = 1 decade
100 years = 1 century

Metric Units Charts

Length
1 km = 1,000 m
1 m = 10 dm
1 m = 100 cm
1 m = 1,000 mm
1 dm = 10 cm
1 cm = 10 mm

Weight
1 metric ton = 1,000 kg
1 kg = 1,000 g
1 g = 1,000 mg

Capacity
1 kL = 1,000 L
1 L = 1,000 mL

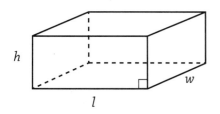

Volume = $l \times w \times h$

Fraction Strips up to Twelfths

1 Whole

$\frac{1}{2}$	$\frac{1}{2}$

$\frac{1}{3}$	$\frac{1}{3}$	$\frac{1}{3}$

$\frac{1}{4}$	$\frac{1}{4}$	$\frac{1}{4}$	$\frac{1}{4}$

$\frac{1}{5}$	$\frac{1}{5}$	$\frac{1}{5}$	$\frac{1}{5}$	$\frac{1}{5}$

$\frac{1}{6}$	$\frac{1}{6}$	$\frac{1}{6}$	$\frac{1}{6}$	$\frac{1}{6}$	$\frac{1}{6}$

$\frac{1}{8}$	$\frac{1}{8}$	$\frac{1}{8}$	$\frac{1}{8}$	$\frac{1}{8}$	$\frac{1}{8}$	$\frac{1}{8}$	$\frac{1}{8}$

$\frac{1}{10}$	$\frac{1}{10}$	$\frac{1}{10}$	$\frac{1}{10}$	$\frac{1}{10}$	$\frac{1}{10}$	$\frac{1}{10}$	$\frac{1}{10}$	$\frac{1}{10}$	$\frac{1}{10}$

$\frac{1}{12}$	$\frac{1}{12}$	$\frac{1}{12}$	$\frac{1}{12}$	$\frac{1}{12}$	$\frac{1}{12}$	$\frac{1}{12}$	$\frac{1}{12}$	$\frac{1}{12}$	$\frac{1}{12}$	$\frac{1}{12}$	$\frac{1}{12}$

GRADES 2–6
TEST PRACTICE
for Common Core

With Common Core Standards being implemented across America, it's important to give students, teachers, and parents the tools they need to achieve success. That's why Barron's has created the *Core Focus* series. These multi-faceted, grade-specific workbooks are designed for self-study learning, and the units in each book are divided into thematic lessons that include:

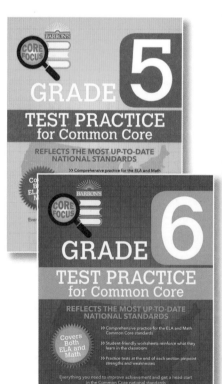

- Specific, focused practice through a variety of exercises, including multiple-choice, short answer, and extended response questions

- A unique scaffolded layout that organizes questions in a way that challenges students to apply the standards in multiple formats

- "Fast Fact" boxes and a cumulative assessment in Mathematics and English Language Arts (ELA) to help students increase knowledge and demonstrate understanding across the standards

Perfect for in-school or at-home study, these engaging and versatile workbooks will help students meet and exceed the expectations of the Common Core.

Grade 2 Test Practice for Common Core
Maryrose Walsh and Judith Brendel
ISBN 978-1-4380-0550-8
Paperback, $14.99, *Can$16.99*

Grade 3 Test Practice for Common Core
Renee Snyder, M.A. and Susan M. Signet, M.A.
ISBN 978-1-4380-0551-5
Paperback, $14.99, *Can$16.99*

Grade 4 Test Practice for Common Core
Kelli Dolan and Shephali Chokshi-Fox
ISBN 978-1-4380-0515-7
Paperback, $14.99, *Can$16.99*

Grade 5 Test Practice for Common Core
Lisa M. Hall and Sheila Frye
ISBN 978-1-4380-0595-9
Paperback, $14.99, *Can$16.99*

Grade 6 Test Practice for Common Core
Christine R. Gray and Carrie Meyers-Herron
ISBN 978-1-4380-0592-8
Paperback, $14.99, *Can$16.99*

Barron's Educational Series, Inc.
250 Wireless Blvd.
Hauppauge, N.Y. 11788
Order toll-free: 1-800-645-3476

In Canada:
Georgetown Book Warehouse
34 Armstrong Ave.
Georgetown, Ontario L7G 4R9
Canadian orders: 1-800-247-7160

Prices subject to change without notice.

Coming soon to your local book store or visit **www.barronseduc.com**

(#295 R11/14)